The Evolution of the AMERICAN GOSPEL by Arthur Bailey

Arthur Bailey

The Evolution of the **American Gospel**
By Arthur Bailey
Arthur Bailey Ministries
PO Box 49744
Charlotte, NC 28277

Published and Produced in the United States of America
By Higher Heart Productions LLC for Arthur Bailey Ministries
ISBN: 978-1-5480494-0-9
Library of Congress Control Number: 2017945453

For more information visit www.ArthurBaileyMinistries.com

This book is designed to compliment Arthur Bailey Ministries videos and/or published teachings. Words in brackets [ ] are typically added for clarification by the editor and publisher.

★ **Table Of Contents** ★

★ Table Of Contents ★

Part Four (continued)

Part Five 167

Part Six 203

★ **Part One** ★

We are going to be talking about a topic that I have been thinking about and working on and pondering for quite some time. I'm just trying to figure out how to bring it forth; and of course there is the timing of bringing it forth. It is called *The Evolution of the American Gospel.*

What we are going to see is how we have been impacted and how the world has been affected by the gospel that originated in America. You would think that because the gospel is a biblical doctrine, that it originated in the Bible. The *true* Gospel of the Kingdom certainly did. The American Gospel originated in America. We're going to look at that.

This is something that has been on me for some time. The more I have traveled and the more we have taken missionary trips and journeys to places like Israel, Russia, Ukraine and other places; I have noticed where people are using the Bible in the language that it has been translated into for them. I have spoken to individuals who, based on their translation of the book, have taken positions on certain doctrinal issues; even when some of those positions have been contrary to Scripture.

It became apparent to me on my first missionary trip to Israel. I encountered Israelis who had an Israeli-Hebrew translation of the American English Bible. I remember my thoughts, among which were:

> *"How is it that these Hebrew people have a Bible from America that is translated into Hebrew?"*

What made me begin to think along those lines was that these Israelis were having church services, worship services just like the American churches. The doctrines that came from America are now permeating the Israeli congregations. I don't know about you, but my understanding is that the gospel originated in Israel. That's my understanding and also that from Israel, the gospel was to go "to the nations."

What I came face to face with was an American Gospel in the land of the Hebrews. It was a gospel that didn't come from Israel. It was a gospel that came from America.

Israel's Gospel vs. America's Gospel

What is the difference between the gospel that came from Israel and the gospel that came from America?

Is there a difference? I have to tell you that there are a lot of differences. We are going to look at some of those differences today.

When I think about the word "gospel," it used to be that one thought came to mind. That's when I was just a believer in "Jesus." When I was a believer in Jesus and I heard the gospel, it was "the Gospel of Jesus Christ," so "the gospel" only had one meaning for me. But the more I've searched and the more I've studied, the more I have found the gospel to be confusing to various people. In fact, it is that *confused gospel* that has created divisions among people, and that has established denominations.

When I read the Bible, I don't see Pentecostals and Baptists and Methodists and Presbyterians. I do see in the gospels – there we go. We've got the Gospel of *Mark*, the Gospel of *Matthew*, the Gospel of *Luke* and the Gospel of *John*. We've got four different gospels right there. We know that when Paul is writing, the Bible speaks of him saying "according to my gospel." Then he talks about "another" gospel.

On top of that, I read the gospel messages. I see the Gospel of Jesus Christ, the Gospel of God and the Gospel of the Kingdom. There was a Baptist Gospel in my first church. There was the Charismatic Pentecostal Apostolic Faith Gospel in my next church. There was the Lutheran Gospel, the "Full" Gospel and the Reformed Gospel. Over a period of time then and when I hear "gospel" now, I want to ask:

"What gospel are you talking about?"

You see, I don't have just one idea of "gospel" now. I've got a lot of them. When I'm dealing with people about the gospel, I realize in the conversation that you're talking about one gospel and I'm talking about a different gospel. So first of all, we need to know what gospel we are talking about if we are going to continue the conversation.

This stretches our intellect. It stretches our spiritual mind. It causes us to begin to become more specific and to drill down. The more specific and drilled down that we go, the less confusion there is. There's a lot of confusion, so we're going to spend some time talking about *The Evolution of the American Gospel*.

I'm going to try to lay sound groundwork and a foundation here, but I think that you already have kind of an idea of all of the different definitions or associations that emerge or show up in conversations when the word "gospel" comes about.

I want to tell you what you should expect in this teaching series. I want you to know what you should gain from the teaching and what you should have after we're done. In this series of teachings, you will be able to identify and distinguish:

- The Gospel of YeHoVaH/God
- The Gospel of Yeshua/Jesus
- The Gospel of the Kingdom of God

I will tell you right now that all of those gospels are one and the same. They are just said several ways. I wonder:

> *"Why did the translator use one particular definition instead of so many different usages of the gospel?"*

For instance, why say "the Gospel of YeHoVaH" or "the Gospel of God" if it is the "Gospel of Jesus" or if the Gospel of Jesus or Yeshua is the Gospel of the Kingdom? What I read is this. I read the Gospel of God, the Gospel of Jesus or the Gospel of the Kingdom. It's hard for me to come to the same conclusion because it's the use of different words, but they're the same gospel.

Now, maybe all of your minds don't work like mine, but I have been forced to think a certain way. That is because I have not called myself to ministry. I have been *called to* the ministry. People look to me to have answers, which means that I have to find answers to help people walk their walk. That's what I've been called to do.

For a person who hasn't been called to do certain things, they can casually read the Bible and just figure stuff out and come to certain conclusions; even though their conclusions may be incorrect. That's because all they are going to do is have conversations with people. A whole lot of people are not necessarily looking to them for answers to biblical questions or for doctrinal understanding.

This is why people can get into conversations and have all kinds of conversations. The conversations can go over and over and over and around and around and around. But when I'm done with the conversation, I want to have accomplished something. I don't want to just talk for the sake of talking.

I've been in too many conversations where there's a whole lot of talking but no action. By the time the conversation is over, we're no further ahead than we were when we first started the conversation. It is like:

> *"You know, I just don't have that kind of time any more."*

Halleluyah.

- You will know what the Synoptic Gospels are.

I put this in the next section, but what I want to do is this. I'm going to jump. I'm going to do something that I don't normally do. I think I need to do it.

Synoptic Gospels

How many of you have ever heard the term "Synoptic Gospels?"

8

Those of you who have studied and read are going to hear this term. The "Synoptic Gospels" really embody three gospel writings. They are the Gospel of *Matthew*, the Gospel of *Luke* and the Gospel of *Mark*. *John* is not part of the Synoptic Gospels; which is another gospel term – the Synoptic Gospels. It is like:

> *"Is the Synoptic Gospel a different gospel than the other gospels?"*

The Synoptic Gospels are called that because *Matthew*, *Mark* and *Luke* generally have the same stories, although they may be arranged a little differently and the wording may be slightly different. That's of course because neither Mark nor Luke were eyewitnesses of Yeshua. The only gospel writers who were eyewitnesses of Yeshua were Matthew and John. Naturally there are those who question who John was.

I'm not trying to throw anything out there or confuse you any further. I know that you all are not confused [speaking to the audience], but the Synoptic Gospels don't include *John*. It only includes *Matthew, Mark* and *Luke*. It is believed that *Mark* was written before *Matthew*; even though *Matthew* comes before *Mark*. It is also believed that *Matthew* and *Luke* pulled from *Mark*.

These thoughts are from theologians who have had conversations based on how these gospel writings are arranged. Some time ago when we were doing the *Discipleship Training* course, I put something out there that I really never thought about until I was faced with the idea that there are a lot of writings that didn't get into the book that we call the Bible.

Having access to the 1611 King James and the New King James Bibles (or the King James that came after 1611); it was easy to compare the two and to see that there were writings in one that were missing from the other.

To think that all of my life I have been taught that this Bible is "the unadulterated, infallible word of YeHoVaH." **It is**

inspired. I'm assuming that in the days of sermons in the 1611 era that they probably held up their Bible and said:

> *"This is the infallible, inspired, unadulterated word of YeHoVaH."*

We learned in Seminary about the whole canon, the process of measuring whether or not a particular book was inspired by the Holy Spirit, and that the responsibility was given to individuals to make those determinations. Between the 1611 group and the later group who decided that the 1611 group wasn't as inspired; I'm trying to figure it out.

Listen folks. Here's what I'm trying to do. **I don't have time to play religious games. I don't have time to play "church."** I spent a lot of my life out there in the world, trying to figure stuff out. I've come into the things of faith to see that there are a lot of games. There is a lot of manipulation. There are a lot of denominations. There are a lot of beliefs. There are a lot of disagreements. **All I'm trying to do is find the truth.** That's it!

I'm not trying to make alliances. I'm not trying to climb some religious denominational corporate ladder. I'm just trying to find the truth so that I can live this thing out. I'm only interested in living it out with people who want to live out the truth. What about all of the other ones? I don't have time for it. There have been people in my life. I have had to cut them off. I have had to say:

> *"Do you know what? I have wasted enough time with you! I've had enough conversations with you."*

Our path separated some time ago. If you look me up or if you find something on *Facebook* or you find out where I'm at and you want to call and try to catch up, I'm going to tell you where I'm at. If you don't want to be there, there isn't any catching up to do. I'll catch you up to where I am.

But if you want me to catch up to where you are and you are still doing some of the things that you were doing, listen. There are a lot of people out there that you can relate with and be

10

friends with and have fellowship with. Our fellowship is not going to last too long unless I come to the conclusion that you are as serious about this walk as I am. That's all I'm trying to do, folks.

I don't have time for all of that other stuff. One of these days I'm going to have to stand before my Master. You all aren't him. Do you hear what I'm saying? I am saying one of these days. There's no time for:

"Uh, uh, but, uh uh, well, uh uh..."

Nope. There's no time for that. So when it came down to all of this, I had to come to the conclusion that this book that we call the Bible had been given to us by individuals who have translated it and used transliteration in the process of translation and have added words. One reason is because some words don't translate.

I could never understand why they put "Easter" in there. I see certain things in the Bible that say to me that there are some folks who are trying to fool me. If I don't search this thing out a little differently, I'm going to start following my Messiah in a **paganistic, idolatrous manner.** I didn't leave the world to get caught up in another world called "religion." I'm trying to walk my faith out.

Dating the Synoptic Gospels		
MARK MATTHEW · LUKE **ASSUMPTION A** Matthew and Luke used Mark as a major source **View No.1** Mark written in the 50s or early 60s A.D. (1) Matthew written in late 50s or the 60s (2) Luke written 59–63 **View No.2** Mark written 65–70 (1) Matthew written in the 70s or later (2) Luke written in the 70s or later	MATTHEW | MARK | LUKE **ASSUMPTION B** Matthew and Luke did not use Mark as a source **View No.1** Mark could have been written anytime between 50 and 70 **View No.2** Mark written 65–70 (1) Matthew written in the 50s (see Introduction to Matthew: Date and Place of Writing) (2) Luke written 59–63 (see Introduction to Luke: Date and Place of Writing)	

This Synoptic Gospels have several assumptions. As you can see, there is Assumption A. In that one, *Matthew* and *Luke* used *Mark* as a major source. That's view number 1; that it was written between the late 50s and the 60s AD.

```
     MARK  ═══════╗
                   ╚════╗              ╗
               MATTHEW              LUKE
ASSUMPTION A
Matthew and Luke used Mark as a major source

View No. 1  Mark written in the 50s or early 60s A.D.
     (1) Matthew written in late 50s or the 60s
     (2) Luke written 59–63

View No. 2  Mark written 65–70
     (1) Matthew written in the 70s or later
     (2) Luke written in the 70s or later
```

Some people say:

> *"I don't care when it was written. It's in the Bible and that's all that I need! It's what the word says and that's enough for me. The Bible says it and that's enough."*

Do you know what I'm saying? You've probably heard of people like that.

> *"If the word says it..."*

We have to conclude that there is some stuff in here that YeHoVaH didn't say. When we began to deal with the "red letter" edition, that's when it all came out. The red letter edition has the words of Yeshua as far as the gospel is saying. It is as if everybody wants to get the red letter edition. I had my red letter edition.

One day it dawned on me. Whose words are in black? It's a logical question! If the words of Yeshua are in red, then that means that the stuff in black are words that he didn't say. So, who said it? Now I can begin to compare their notes with the notes of other writers to see if there is a consistency.

That's because if there are two or three witnesses, I can work with that. But where there is no witness, I have more questions. Are you following me? This is not to nit-pick.

I've been fooled. My parents have been fooled. My grandparents were fooled. There has been a lot of fooling! I can continue down the fool's way or I can get wisdom and knowledge and understanding which are only going to come from the one who gave us this book.

"He ain't no fool and he doesn't make fools."

The reason that people get fooled is because they are following religion claiming to be following him.

"I'm going to follow him. That's who I need."

I realized that Noah didn't have a Bible. Abraham didn't have a Bible and Moses didn't have a Bible; yet these individuals walked with YeHoVaH.

There is the possibility folks, that we can walk with YeHoVaH, but then people get Bibles and then they want to get all "literal" in their interpretation. You know:

"It doesn't literally mean that. This is what it literally means..."

It is like:

"Where are you getting your 'literal' meanings from?"

What are you searching? What materials? What tools are you using to come to that conclusion? When I was in Seminary, you had PhDs in Theology in one Seminary. I go to another one and you have PhDs in another Seminary. If you are in another denomination, you've got PhDs in that denomination and theology. All of these PhDs do not agree and they are all well-learned men! Right? Do you hear what I'm saying? So it is like:

"Who can I trust? Who can I trust to tell me the truth?"

It is obvious that I can't trust men. Yeshua didn't. **So I'm going to look to the one that he looked to.** When I look to him and I start looking to some others, it is like:

"You all aren't saying the same thing that he's saying. Maybe I'm not hearing. Maybe my hearing needs to be adjusted."

13

I have seen in the word, things that I thought I understood and walked in, only to find out later that I didn't have an understanding. When I have that kind of situation, what do I do? I don't try to defend that. I repent from that. When you know better, you do better. That's called growing.

MATTHEW	MARK	LUKE

ASSUMPTION B

Matthew and Luke did not use Mark as a source

View No. 1 Mark could have been written anytime between 50 and 70

View No. 2 Mark written 65–70
  (1) Matthew written in the 50s (see Introduction to Matthew: Date and Place of Writing)
  (2) Luke written 59–63 (see Introduction to Luke: Date and Place of Writing)

Assumption B or the second view is that *Mark* was written between 65 and 70 AD. *Matthew* was written in the 70s AD. *Luke* was written in the 70s or later. In Assumption B, *Matthew* and *Luke* did not use *Mark* as a source. *Mark* could have been written any time between view number 1 (50 and 70 AD) or View 2, that *Mark* was written between 65 and 70 AD.

You've heard me say that when we begin to study a book, you want to see who wrote it, to whom it was written, why it was written and when. These are some of the tools that are used to determine the authenticity of any writings.

If Mark died at a certain age and later on some books emerge with Marks' name on them, then I have to ask if Mark wrote that. You know? We have books from individuals like Enoch. There are now books out there with his name on it. For example, there are the Apostles' Creeds that none of the apostles had anything to do with.

There is a lot of theology going on. If you've sat in the school of theology at the feet of the theologians, then you subscribe to their doctrines and follow their paths. Most of us didn't have a say in the matter. We were born this way. We were born into our faith. You went to the same church your Momma or your Daddy went to or whoever took you to church, right?

By the time you got to think for yourself (for real), you already had foundations established in you. These were religious foundations that affected how you saw the world. Coming into the Hebrew Roots, we come to a place where we acknowledge that we saw some stuff wrong. We moved from Sunday (which we grew up in) to keeping the Sabbath.

We have come to realize that the Law did change. We see the change that took place and what is applicable today from what is not applicable. We have come to realize the role that Yeshua and the New Testament play in our understanding of how to live our lives out as believers and followers of Messiah.

That's what I want to try to help us with while I'm being helped. That's because **when you know the truth, what happens? There's freedom.** The freer you are, the more you realize the less you have to try to defend yourself. I can't stand here defending myself claiming that he is my defender!

He is the one who is fighting for me. He's the one who is defending me. All I have to do is walk out what he reveals to me. If others around me don't understand that, then I can do my best to try to explain it.

But with some people, no matter what you say, you are not going to be able to help them to understand. They just won't get it because they don't want to get it, for some reason; and for other reasons, maybe it isn't time. I don't know.

You are going to understand and distinguish the Gospel of YeHoVaH and Yeshua and the Kingdom; which you have already come to realize.

- You will know what the Synoptic Gospels are.

This is what we just talked about.

- You will know what Paul's Gospel is.

We will deal with that.

- You will know what other Gospels are.
- You will know what the Everlasting Gospel is.
- You will know and understand what the *true* Gospel is.
- You will be able to distinguish the difference between:
  1. The Gospel of Yeshua/Jesus (the gospel Yeshua/Jesus preached)

Yes, there is a difference.

And you will be able to understand:

  2. The gospel about Yeshua/Jesus

- You will understand how the gospel that Yeshua preached became the Gospel of Jesus Christ.
- You will be able to identify the danger and pitfalls of the American Gospel.
- You will learn how the Hebrew Gospel message EVOLVED into the American Gospel and witness the evolution.
- You will understand what I mean when I say "Hebrew Roots Gospel" and why returning to our Hebrew Roots Gospel is so important to our faith (because it is correct knowledge).

There is knowledge, and there is *correct* knowledge.

- You will be able to truly appreciate our salvation, the one who brought us salvation, and the gospel message of salvation.
- You will be better equipped to understand and proclaim the *true* Gospel of Yeshua. (That is the gospel Yeshua preached).
- You will understand the Hebrew Roots of the gospel, the foundation of the gospel, the message of the gospel, and so much more.

There is stuff that you are going to understand that is not included in any of these bullet points.

Webster's [Dictionary] definition of "evolution" is: one of a set of prescribed movements: a process of change in a certain direction. That's the definition of evolution, based on Webster's.

The Evolution of the American Gospel

Let's begin. We're going to start in *Mark,* dealing with the Evolution of the American Gospel.

> *Mark 1:1 – "The **beginning** of the **gospel** of Yeshua Messiah, the son of El [God];"*

The Son of Elohim. This word "beginning" in the Greek is: "*arche,*" which means: origin.

If you notice, *Mark* opens up with the beginning, the origin of the gospel. It is dealing with a person or thing that commences, the first person or thing in a series, the leader; that by which anything begins to be, the origin, the active cause. It also means: the extremity of a thing. Then it goes off into the corners of a sail; the first place, principality, rule or magistracy; of angels and demons.

The usage of the word "beginning" is this. It is used forty times, but in other places it is called "principality" (this word "*arche*") eight times. It is twice used as "corner" and "first."

He is talking about the beginning of the gospel. We are going to look at the Greek. Later on we're going to look at the Hebrew. With the word "*gospel*" you are going to find that the word itself is not found in the Old Testament, but it originated there.

The problem that I have found, especially with people who have Concordances and some different tools and notes, is this. Let me just share some things with you that I have noticed. It really didn't make a big difference until I started looking at things from a Hebrew Roots perspective. One of the things that I noticed was that in Bible College, the focus was on the Greek portions of the Scriptures and not the Hebrew. At the time, it was no big deal.

That's because Jesus "wasn't in" the Old Testament and all I wanted to focus on was Jesus. I was being taught to teach Jesus to a people who believe in Jesus, so that's where it didn't really matter. But also the tools, the Bible tools, the online tools and the electronic [hand held] tools, the disks and the library that you develop are important. I looked and some Hebrew words are not as clearly defined as are the Greek words.

I also noticed very clearly that there were words used in the Greek portion of the Bible that weren't used in the Hebrew portion of the Bible and which originated in the Hebrew portion of the Bible. I acknowledged and identified that the Greek Bible seemed to be totally distinct from the Hebrew portion of the Bible. It never really dawned on me. I never thought much of it until I started searching the Hebrew Roots of my faith.

This word "gospel" in the Greek is: "*euaggelion.*" You won't find this word in the Hebrew portion of the Bible. You'll find another word that we'll discuss later, but this word evolved from there. It took on a totally different identity than the original. It's difficult to make that connection from the New [Testament and] connecting it to the Old [Testament]. Based on the New, it is as if it doesn't even exist.

Another word that you won't find in its name form is the word "Jesus." You won't find "Jesus" in the Old Testament, but he's littered throughout the New Testament. This leads some people to believe that Jesus didn't exist until *Matthew,* when the entire Old Testament (and none of these individuals would disagree) points to him.

It points to him, but his name is not mentioned. The translators decided to put "Emmanuel" and "Wonderful Counselor" when the fact is that **his name *is* there. It's just hidden**. If you don't know where to look, you won't find it!

This word "*euaggelion*" means: a reward for good tidings. How many of you automatically say:

"Blessed are they who bring good news? How beautiful are the feet of them that bring good news."

You see, there is "gospel," but it is not called the gospel. The word here says what? A reward for good tidings; good tidings; the glad tidings of the Kingdom of Elohim soon to be set up. That's *soon* to be set up. It is like:

"You all, he set up his Kingdom from the beginning!"

But if you let these guys tell it, he's not going to set it up until *after* Jesus died. Right? The usage of the word "gospel" is forty-six times as the gospel, eleven times as the Gospel of Christ; Gospel of God seven times and the Gospel of the Kingdom three times. It's the same word.

Yeshua is the salvation of YeHoVaH first preached (or should I say) announced by Jacob in *Genesis 49:18*. Here is what it says:

Genesis 49:18 – "I have waited for thy ___salvation___, O ___LORD___."

That's the King James Version. The word there, "salvation" is what? "Yeshua" [Yeshuwah]. I have waited for Yeshua. Now, that's the translation of the word "salvation" in that passage, but you see salvation. Here's what this is going to point to. Who is our salvation? Nobody argues that.

He IS our salvation. So he is our salvation, but there were those who didn't know him by that name; or get this. If Jacob spoke Hebrew (and he is speaking Hebrew), here is what he said:

"Oh, I have waited for your Yeshua, YeHoVaH."

That's what he would be saying! He wouldn't have used the word "salvation" because salvation is translated into Hebrew and he was speaking Hebrew. **He would have used the Hebrew.** Right? **He would have been speaking YESHUA, wouldn't he?**

Yeshua is salvation, deliverance, and welfare. I'm not talking about government welfare, but the government of his Kingdom. You see, I don't mind being on the welfare system of his Kingdom. [Laughter and agreement by the audience] If I get desperate enough, I'll take some welfare from Uncle Sam. I'm just putting it out there. My pride (if it still exists) will not let me go hungry when somebody is saying:

> *"Here is some food. Take this EBT. Take this food stamp."*[1]

If the food stamp goes to the grocery store [after you spend it] and I'm hungry, what am I supposed to do, die? Would you die? I'm not dying. Pride will not take me to my grave. But the welfare of his Kingdom: salvation, deliverance, welfare, prosperity; salvation (by God); victory. All of these words are tied.

Yeshua is my deliverance. Yeshua is my salvation. Yeshua is my victory. Yeshua is my welfare. Yeshua is my prosperity. He's my help. He's my health. He's my saving, my Savior.

This is what Jacob is saying. That word "YHVH" or "Jehovah" [YeHoVaH] meaning "the existing One"; is the proper name of the one true God/Elohim; unpronounced except with the vowel pointings of [Strong's 0136].

Some people say "Yod-Hey-Vav-Hey," which is what we have here [YHVH]. I have to get a better translation of Hebrew lettering because as you can see from here, we've got the vowel pointings that are not included in the "YHVH." [Arthur points to a wall hanging behind him that has the Hebrew name on it with the vowel pointings.]

How many of you know that "YHVH" is nobody's name? People are saying:

---

[1] EBT is an American welfare benefit transfer card system which provides food purchasing benefits to recipients of the program.

"Oh, I thank you Yod-Hey-Vav-Hey."

It's like:

"Really?"

Then you ought to say:

"Well, I thank you A-R-T-H-U-R or A-T-H-R."

My name is not "A-T-H-R." I know you guys have this text stuff going on where you just shorten everything. [Arthur makes hand gestures like he is texting on an imaginary cell phone.]

Yeshua was also announced by Moses in *Exodus 14* and *15*. This is what it says:

> *Exodus 14:13 – "And Moses said unto the people, 'Fear ye not, stand still, and see the* **Yeshua** *[salvation] of* **YeHoVaH** *[the LORD], which he will shew you to day: for the Egyptians whom ye have seen to day, ye shall see them again no more for ever.'"*

Then he says:

> *Exodus 15:2-3 – "***YeHoVaH** *[the LORD] is my strength and song, and he is become my* **Yeshua** *[salvation]: he is my Elohim [God], and I will prepare him an habitation; my father's El [God], and I will exalt him.* ³**YeHoVaH** *[the LORD] is a man of war:* **YeHoVaH** *[the LORD] is his name."*

He is a man of war. He is going to fight for you. You see, we have to learn to truly let him do the fighting. If we really let him do the fighting, do you know what we avoid? We avoid strife. We avoid contention. We avoid high blood pressure. We avoid a lot of health issues that come when we get all worked up. And then we say [shouting in mock anger]:

> *"I'm not going to fight you! The LORD fights my battles!!!"*

It's like:

21

"Well, what do you call that?"

You see, some people fight with words and we talk about "waiting on him" while fighting. That is the author of confusion. We have to learn. The Bible says that where there is strife and where there is contention, there is confusion and every evil work. So wherever there is strife and contention, there is confusion. Strife can hurt you pretty badly. It can mess with your organs, your system, your brain, your heart, and your vitals.

You don't want to be in strife. You certainly don't want to operate in confusion. That's because when you're in that camp, you're in the camp of the enemy. How are you going to go and take something out of the enemy's camp when you've got some stuff that belongs to him? You go over there for a fight and you end up in jail. That word again, "Yeshua" means salvation, deliverance and welfare and then YeHoVaH.

Back to *Mark.*

> *Mark 1:1 – "The beginning of the gospel of* **_Yeshua Messiah_** *[Jesus Christ], the Son of Elohim [God]."*

Here's what I want to point out. This word "Jesus" we know. We found it in Yeshua. That's the name we use. In the Greek it is "*Iesous*" [ee-ay-sooce']. That word is supposed to mean: "Jesus" = "Jehovah is salvation." Another definition is "Joshua." Some people say that the word "Jesus" came from the Hebrew origin of Joshua and that the name is "*Yehowshuwa*'" [yeh-ho-shoo'-ah] or Yehowshu'a (Yehoshua).

When people say "*Yehoshua*," they mean "*Yeshua*" or they mean "YeHoVaH is salvation." But people who use the name "Jesus" say and think that that is what it means as well. Yet we know that **"Jesus" is certainly not the name his mother named him.**

That's because "Jesus" is neither Latin nor Greek. It isn't Hebrew. It's not even Old English. It's Modern English! Anyone who has a 1611 King James Bible knows that the 1611 King

22

James Bible is Old English; which is an Anglo-Saxon English that evolved into what we know of today as American English.

When you try to read that Anglo-Saxon English like you try to read through the King James Bible, you'd probably get through a few verses before you put that down and pick up something that you can read and understand. That's because it's a little difficult, but that's how people spoke. We don't speak that way today. Why? Because we have what? Evolved. When we evolve into, we evolve away from. Do you hear what I'm saying? That's why we're calling this *The Evolution of the American Gospel.*

So Joshua or Yehoshua or Yeshua is salvation. YeHoVaH is salvation. As a definition, it gives "son of Nun." Now, the word *"Christos"* [khris-tos] means: Christ = anointed. It also means: Christ was the Messiah, the Son of God; anointed.

Some of you noticed when I showed you in *John 4* when the woman said:

> *"We know that when Messiah comes (which being interpreted is called 'Christ')..."*

It is basically:

> *"We know Christ is coming (being interpreted is called 'Christ')."*

Why are you giving Messiah a name by evolving him into "Christ" (which is "anointed"), when in actuality "Messiah" is a much broader term than "anointed?" Messiah, King, Priest, Savior; Messiah is all of that. He's not just anointed but King, Priest and Savior.

Yeshua, the salvation of YeHoVaH, is the literal gospel. Literally, **Yeshua is salvation.** Yeshua, the literal gospel, also preached the gospel. So when Yeshua was teaching, he was the gospel and he was preaching the gospel.

What was he preaching about? Himself.

That's what he was preaching about. The gospel was saying:

"Listen. If you want to be saved, you have to believe in me."

He was talking to a people who said:

"You must be out of your mind! We believe in God!"

Then when Yeshua said:

"You know, well, you're looking at him. If you believe in him, you would believe in me because if you've seen him, you've seen me. He and me are one."

"What?!"

[Laughter] People had a real problem with that! I suspect that the people had a real problem with that because it's easier to believe in one that you can't see; especially if he isn't talking and he doesn't talk. So we interpret what we think he is saying and we can "rely" upon our own interpretation. Do you hear this? Now one comes and says:

"Listen. You all can't rely upon your own interpretation. Let me tell you what he said. Let me tell you what he means. That's why I'm here. I'm here to save you."

"We're already saved! We don't need you!"

That is what they're saying.

Yeshua the gospel. Verse 14:

Mark 1:14 – "Now after that John was put in prison, Yeshua came into Galilee, preaching the gospel of the kingdom of Elohim,"

So the gospel was preaching the gospel. That's the simplest way of saying it. **The message of the gospel declared that Yeshua is the salvation of YeHoVaH.** That's the message. The forerunner of this message was pronounced by the prophet.

*Mark 1:2 – "**As it is written in the prophets,** Behold, I send my messenger before thy face, which shall prepare thy way before thee."*

Mark 1:3 – "The voice of one crying in the wilderness, 'Prepare ye the way of the Lord, make his paths straight.'"

This is prophesied. This is coming "as it is written." Remember that when you see "as it is written," that you want to find out where it is written. This is how you compare Scriptures. This is how you search Scriptures. This is how you are a Berean. Bereans search the Scriptures to see. I want you to see this. The Bible says that the Bereans searched the Scriptures, right? What did they search? People say:

"I'm a Berean!"

It is like:

"If you were a Berean, you would be searching the Scriptures the Bereans searched."

Now, Paul is coming to preach the gospel, right? If Paul was preaching something other than what the Scriptures said, when they searched the Scriptures, they wouldn't have found Paul's teachings. When they searched the Scriptures, they were searching the Old Testament. What was Paul preaching from? **Paul was preaching Messiah from the Old Testament!** Why?

Yeshua said to the Pharisees:

"Search the Scriptures, for therein they speak of me. Do you think you have salvation? Search! You're rejecting salvation!"

That's what he's saying to them.

"Your salvation is looking you straight in your face and trying to show you the way."

So when he says:

"I am the way. I am the path. I am salvation personified..."

Are you getting this? That comes from *Isaiah 40.*

> *Isaiah 40:3 – "The voice of him that crieth in the wilderness, 'Prepare ye the way of the LORD,'"*

Prepare ye the way of YeHoVaH.

> *"'...make straight in the desert a highway for our Elohim.'"*

Then *Mark* goes on to say:

> *Mark 1:4 – "John did baptize in the wilderness, and **preach** <u>the baptism of repentance for the remission of **sins**.</u>"*

Now we get to see what John was preaching. We are going to see that Yeshua starts preaching what John was preaching after John was put in prison. What was John preaching? He was preaching **the baptism of repentance.** John was preaching the gospel as the forerunner of Messiah; preparing the way for Messiah. When John was put away, Yeshua began to preach. He picked up where John was preaching.

> *"Repent, for the Kingdom of Heaven is at hand! Repent!"*

Repent from what?

Sin.

We're going to look at this in a moment, but this word that he says, "preach" is "*kerusso*" in the Greek. It means: to be a herald, to officiate as a herald; to proclaim after the manner of a herald; always with the suggestion of formality, gravity and an authority which must be listened to and obeyed; to publish, proclaim openly: something which has been done. It is used fifty-one times as "preach," five times as "publish," twice as "proclaimed" and as "preached" and "preacher."

The reason why I am pointing this out is because what we have here is the messenger and the message. It is one who proclaims the message and the message one proclaims.

Sometimes people confuse the messenger with the message. You see, **if we can discredit the messenger, we can reject the message.** Again, if we can discredit the messenger, we can reject the message.

How do you discredit the message? You find flaws. You find a problem. Think about how we do that. When somebody comes to us — I do it. I have to reject that because the thought is automatic. When somebody comes to me to correct me, I can think of probably a dozen things that I can throw back at them. It is like:

> *"You know, you're coming to tell me about myself..."*

And do you know a good passage? [Arthur paraphrases.]

> *"Before you come to tell me about the moat in my eye brother, you need to take that big old log out of your own eye."*

Do you see how we do that? We can find a problem with the person who is pointing stuff out to us and the question is, why? Why do we do that? It is because we don't want to hear what they have to say.

Now, the sad thing is that what they have to say (if it is of him) is for our good. That says that we choose stuff that is against that which is good. When the Almighty sends stuff to us that is for our good, by discrediting the messenger, we can discredit the message which is supposed to be good for us. When we reject what is good, it never manifests or materializes.

Here is what I have found. I'm asking the Father to do some stuff for me and he wants to do some stuff for me. Right? He wants to do some stuff, but he also knows that if he does what I want him to do; if I don't deal with this and if he does for me what I want him to do, that I'm going to mess it up.

You see, the devil has "dirt" on all of us. Don't think for a moment that the devil doesn't have any dirt on you. He is like politicians during the election cycle. They've got all of their minions out there finding all of the dirt on their opponents. They release a little dirt at certain times, to knock them down. When they get to a certain place, then they release some *WikiLeaks*. They leak some information.

> *"Oh, I didn't know that! I was about to vote for that person! I'm glad I found that out!"*

Right? So the enemy waits until you get to a certain place. You think that your sin isn't going to find you out. Right when you get to that place, here come the blackmailers who know the stuff. Here come the people who are threatening to expose you, so what do you do? You confront the issue in yourself so that when the blackmailers come, they don't have anything to blackmail you with.

How do you do that? Father sends people to you to share things with you that you don't want to hear and you discredit the messenger and keep carrying your blackmailable stuff along with you. So when you now get to that point, you have all of these issues that are arising over stuff that you never dealt with. That keeps you from enjoying what you thought would be most flavorful. Do you see how this stuff works?

This is why you can't look at the messenger before you examine the message. The messenger was John. John was not the message, but here is what the people used. They used religion. This is why the religious leaders asked the messenger if he was the message.

> *"Are you the one? Are you the prophesied Messiah?"*

What did John say? NO! He told them that he (the message) was coming. John answered them, saying:

> *John 1:26 – "I baptize with water: but there standeth one among you, whom ye know not;"*

> *John 1:27 – "He it is, who coming after me is preferred before me, whose shoe's latchet I am not worthy to unloose."*

Don't confuse the message with the messenger. What did he come to do? He came to preach repentance; to proclaim and herald repentance for the remission of sins. You have to understand something folks. The Hebrew people (of all people) had a better understanding of sin than we do.

When you look at Israel, Israel has gone in and out of captivity because of violating YeHoVaH's commands. Because YeHoVaH loves them, he always has a voice, a remnant. He raises up a prophet and sends the prophet to the people to say:

> *"Hey people, you all need to turn back! You all need to repent! You know, I told you in my word that if you don't obey my word, these things are going to happen, so this shouldn't be new to you that you are going into captivity. It's an example. It's a sign that you are walking in disobedience to my word. But if you turn back to me, guess what? I'll turn back to you!"*

When we violate the commands of YeHoVaH, we turn on him. It's not him turning on us. We turn on him and put him in a position where he can't bless us. He can't bless you. You may hear people saying:

> *"I'm blessed in my mess."*

No, you're not! No, you're not! You aren't "blessed" in your mess! **Father doesn't bless mess! He cleans it up!**

The prophets knew that sin put a barrier between the creation and the Creator. Sin keeps Father – it's like Father says:

> *"I want to bless them. I want to bless them! I <u>want</u> to bless them! They won't let me! I WANT to bless them! I've got to get a blessing to them, so here's the plan. Okay, I know you are over there tending your flock, tending your sheep, but I've got...hey...hey, you. Yeah, you. Come here. I've got something for you. I'm going to send you to tell these people."*

"Not me, Lord! Find somebody else!"

"No, I want you to go and tell these people."

"Why?"

"Because I want to bless them, but I can't bless them in the condition they are in. I have to get a message to them. If they would repent, if they would turn and turn to me, then all of these blessings that I want to bless them with, I can bestow upon them before they sin again."

It's like the Father has to try to get in between our sins to get some blessings to us. I believe that he is trying to get in between the last time we sinned and the next time we sin to get some blessings to us so hopefully the blessings will speak to us. Then we'll compare the blessed times when we are walking with him, with the other times when we're not walking with him and say:

"Hey, you know, I just had an epiphany. It seems like life is better when I'm walking in obedience to his word. Go figure!"

What that would hopefully do, is this. An intelligent person, a wise person will make a decision to walk in obedience. That's because curses don't pay. Disobedience doesn't pay. Crime doesn't pay. You see, when you violate the law, that makes you a criminal. When we violate YeHoVaH's Law, that makes us a criminal. Crime doesn't pay.

What did he say about the word "sin?" John came to declare the baptism of repentance for the remission of sins. He says:

"You've got to repent so that your sins will be blotted out, wiped out."

Why? This word "sin" ("*hamartia*") in the Greek is equivalent to (264) and means to be without a share, to miss the mark, to err, to be mistaken, to miss or wander from the path of uprightness and honour, to do or to go wrong. It also means to wander from the Law of God, to violate God's Law. It is that which is done wrong, sin, an offence, a violation of the divine Law in thought or in act.

So when a Hebrew person hears "repent from sin," their first question is:

"What sin?"

The religious leaders say:

"We're not sinners!"

What made the religious leaders sinners? It was one simple violation which led to many more. **That simple violation was adding to – adding to the Law.** YeHoVaH says:

> *"My Law is perfect just the way it is. Don't add anything to it and don't take away from it. Don't diminish it and don't try to hype it up. I'm the one who gave it. I'm the one who knows the interpretation. If my people who know me have the kind of relationship that I want to establish..."*

You see folks, back at Sinai, YeHoVaH's plan was not to write his Law in stones. His plan then was to write his Law in the hearts of men. How? By hearing. **Faith comes by hearing**. YeHoVaH is saying:

> *"You all come up. Let me talk to you all. Let me tell you. Listen. I came. Do you know what? I sent Moses through a lot to bring you all out of Egypt. I promised Abraham that I am going to take you to a land that is a good land. This is a land I have prepared just for you."*

It was similar to how he prepared the Garden [of Eden] for Mr. and Mrs. Adam. It was like everything that they needed would be in the land. They didn't build the houses. They didn't dig the wells. They didn't plant the vineyards. He says:

> *"I'm going to bring you from slavery. I'm going to take you from the bottom of the heap and put you on the top of the hill."*

31

This is what he is doing here. He is taking them from slavery and being looked down on, to being the light of the world and looked up to. This is what the Almighty will do for you, but we have to allow him to have his way in us.

He knows how to take you from wherever you are and put you where he has ordained for you to be. But along the way, he has to get some stuff out of us because we've picked up some stuff before we came to the knowledge of who he is.

Again, we picked up some stuff before we came to the full knowledge of who he is. The stuff that we picked up affects our outlook on him. As a result of that, because the stuff that has happened to many of us has caused us to distrust, we can't for some reason make the distinction between trusting him whom we can't see and men whom we can.

So if we can't trust that which we see, how in the world are we going to trust that which we can't see? This causes us to give lip service. We say that we trust him, but our actions don't show that. All of the things that we've gone through and accumulated, the stuff that people have done to us, men, and all of that stuff is part of that carnal human nature.

When human beings say or do stuff that reminds us of other human beings who did or said things that were similar and who did what they did, it conjures up all of those memories. Because we are not grounded in the word and are probably not wearing tzitzits and are not focused on keeping the commands, those memories cause us to remember that stuff which exalts itself over remembering the word.

We begin to walk in the hurt. We begin to walk in it or to protect ourselves. We begin to guard ourselves and say:

"He is my high tower. He is my fortress."

We don't realize it ladies and gentlemen, but we become accustomed to giving lip service. We convince ourselves with the lip service that we give him that our lip service is genuine and authentic and we believe our own words. I know what I'm talking about.

> *Mark 1:5 – "And there went out unto him all the land of Judaea, and they of Jerusalem, and were all <u>baptized of him in the river of Jordan</u>,"*

Doing what?

> *"... <u>confessing their **sins**</u>."*

For the Gentile today, for the non-Hebrew person today, it is like this. When they say "sin" and when people hear "sin" today; sin in the mind of a church person has evolved from what sin was in the mind of a Hebrew person. When a Hebrew person heard "sin," do you know what came to mind to them? **The Law.**

When a Christian hears "sin," do you know what comes to mind to them? **An act.** We have to look at sin in the context that it is [truly] in.

When I talk about sin, it is not that I'm conscious of sin as much as it is that I am conscious of the Law. I don't want to be one who violates the Law. That's because I know that when I violate his Law, I put this separation [between him and me]. The last thing that I want is to have anything between the Almighty and me. This is why we have to be quick to repent. We have to be quick to hear. We have to be slow to speak. We have to be slow to anger, but this flesh doesn't want to hear that.

Your flesh doesn't want to hear that. I know that my flesh doesn't, so they hear "sin" and they think of "Law." Christians and some Messianics hear "sin" and think of an act. So [the idea is that] I may not be guilty of one thing, but there are some other things that I may be aware of and that I need to work on. The whole point is that I want to work on everything that I am aware of.

But it's painful. That's because to work on these issues means that I have to deal with my flesh. Do you know how you don't like dealing with other peoples' flesh? You certainly don't want to deal with your own. It's easier to deal with other peoples' flesh than with your own flesh. You don't like dealing with other peoples' flesh, so what does that say about you and yours?

I have to work on mine. I have to work on it every day. Father puts people in my life and circumstances and situations that keep me reminded that I have work to do.

> *Mark 1:6-13 – "And John was clothed with camel's hair, and with a girdle of a skin about his loins; and he did eat locusts and wild honey;"*
>
> [7] *"And preached, saying, 'There cometh one mightier than I after me, the latchet of whose shoes I am not worthy to stoop down and unloose.'"*
>
> [8] *"'I indeed have baptized you with water: but he shall baptize you with the Holy Ghost.'"*
>
> [9] *"And it came to pass in those days, that Yeshua came from Nazareth of Galilee, and was baptized of John in Jordan."*
>
> [10] *"And straightway coming up out of the water, he saw the heavens opened, and the Spirit like a dove descending upon him:"*
>
> [11] *"And there came a voice from heaven, saying, 'Thou art my beloved Son, in whom I am well pleased.'"*
>
> [12] *"And immediately the Spirit driveth him into the wilderness."*

Luke tells us that he was driven into the wilderness for what? To be tempted of the devil. *Mark* says:

> [12] *"And immediately the Spirit driveth him into the wilderness."*
>
> [13] *"And he was there in the wilderness forty days, tempted of Satan; and was with the wild beasts; and the angels ministered unto him."*

Luke says that **he was driven into the wilderness to be tempted or he was led into the wilderness to be tempted.** It was not that he was in the wilderness and the devil came to tempt him. It was for the purpose of tempting him. What was the devil's job? It was to cause him to confront that flesh. You might say:

> *"Well, Yeshua didn't have to deal with the flesh."*

Really? You know, get to the point where you see the climax and purpose of his life in the Garden [of Gethsemane] and remember. He was in there praying for three hours. Here's the thing. He prayed for three hours. After the prayer, he did what he was praying that he didn't have to do, so I say that it was three hours for what?

That's because this flesh is something else. This flesh doesn't want to do YeHoVaH's will. That's a lesson we can learn from him. But in the end, it was a three hour prayer that didn't change what he was praying for.

> *Mark 1:14-15 – "Now after that John was put in prison, **Yeshua came into Galilee, preaching the gospel of the Kingdom of Elohim**,"*
>
> [15]*"And saying, 'The time is fulfilled, and the kingdom of Elohim is at hand:'"*

What? You see, here is the gospel in a nutshell, folks.

"Repent ye and believe. Repent ye and believe the gospel."

The American Gospel that is preached in the corporate American churches which identify as Christianity did not originate with Yeshua/Jesus. In fact, what is preached today in the corporate American Westernized church is very different from the gospel that Yeshua/Jesus preached in his day.

The gospel that is being exported from America and that is impacting churches and religious life worldwide is a Western version of the gospel that originated with the Hebrew Messiah called Yeshua.

As I said, as we go through these teachings, what you are going to find is that the things that we deal with today, the gospel message that we're dealing with today has gone through some changes. The gospel that we know today has gone through several phases or transitions. That is for all versions; however you look at them, every last one of them. It doesn't matter which version you have. You can have the closest version there is and it came from something. It came from something.

So here is the evolution and we'll deal with this more later.

1. The Americanized gospel, before it was Americanized, was Westernized.

2. Before it was Westernized, it was Europeanized.

3. Before it was Europeanized, it was Latinized.

4. Before it was Latinized (or Latin), it was Grecized.

5. Before it was Grecized, it was Aramaic and Hebrew.

If you reverse the order, there is the evolution the gospel has gone through. Again, we'll deal with this more a little bit later.

The gospel message has gone from:

1. Hebrew/Aramaic to Greek

2. From Greek to Latin

3. From Latin to European/Westernized (Anglo-Saxon/Old English)

4. From European/Westernized (Anglo-Saxon/Old English) to American English

5. From American English to the various translations of Bibles being shipped around the world

I want to say that I just got a letter. We get several letters from people for Bible translations in their language. We've even gone through the process. This is one of the things that really opened my eyes.

As studied as I am and as knowledgeable as I thought I was; in the process of getting some of our materials translated from English to another language, I learned something. We've got several materials. We've got our book *Sunday Is Not The Sabbath?* that right now is translated into Spanish, Shona, Dutch, Russian and Cebuano [with more on the way].

The point is that these translation processes forced us to look at words we normally wouldn't even be looking at. That was because they were being translated into another language. When they were being translated into another language, as Sisters Simona and PJ were working on it, and Sister Simona was helping to kind of guide this Russian version, we were also translating our *Discipleship Training* program into Russian. I remember some of the conversation she was having with me. I said:

> *"Really? Are you serious?"*

> *"Yes brother. Yes. That word...when you translate it into our language, it doesn't say that."*

So now you have to find the correct word to make it translate properly. It's not that you just go to *Google* and translate "me" and you've got it. It doesn't work that way!

Then you start dealing with the Spanish language like when Sister Rebecca was also working on it and who is from Puerto Rican descent. Then you've got people who speak different dialects other than Puerto Rican who are Spanish and they are looking at it and saying this and that. You have to deal with all of these dialects even though you have a language [that is the same].

I'm thinking back and remembering. This was probably one of the most mind-blowing teaching opportunities that I've ever had. When I went to Kenya the second time and we ended up in Lodwar, which is about thirty miles from the Sudan Desert or the Sudan wilderness, we were there speaking and I had three translators.

I had worked with one. I had even worked with as many as two. But I had to have someone take my English and translate it into Swahili and to take my Swahili and for somebody else to translate it into Kikuyu and to take the Kikuyu and translate it into another language and then have somebody translate it into the local language.

Now I have all of these translations and I don't know what anybody is saying. I am standing there preaching and I have to trust that the translators are translating what I'm saying. This really messed me up: when somebody in the audience corrected the translator! I didn't know that the translator was wrong! Do you hear what I'm saying? When somebody's correcting the translator who's translating for me, it is like:

"Are you really saying what I'm saying?"

Do you understand what I'm saying ladies and gentlemen?

With *The Evolution of the American Gospel*, we're looking at it from where it came from, to [get to] us. We're looking at how it came through that process to [get to] us and how it is now going through another process [as it goes] out from us. Whether you know it or not, **America is the largest exporter of translations of the Bible than any other country.**

The culture is being translated. The doctrine and denominational beliefs are being translated. Do you get this? When we go out to speak to people who have the American version in their language and we're bumping heads; I'm trying to show them that a *Strong's Concordance* does them absolutely no good!

None of the Hebrew tools – no Lexicon, no Concordance will help. That's because those things haven't been translated yet, so all you have is the pure word from their *translation.* And to them, *that's* what it says and you can't show them the Hebrew or the Greek.

Now I'm looking at what we've done as people and how we're affecting others. This is why I would say that out of the hundreds of years – do you know that the gospel that has been in existence, think about this. The gospel that has been in existence for at least nineteen hundred to two thousand years in a world of over seven billion people has only reached about two point five billion. That's in over two thousand years; not to mention the fact that this gospel has been translated and denominationalized. That seems to have caused more division than unity.

This causes me to look at the enormity of the responsibility that we have been given. The enormity of the responsibility that we have been given to take the *true* Gospel of the Kingdom to the ends of the world becomes somewhat overwhelming. That's because I'm thinking that this won't be done in my lifetime.

Maybe I'm wrong, but if it has taken two thousand years to reach two point five billion people, that is not even a third. Well, maybe it's a little over a third of the world's population. That's in over two thousand years. I anticipate that I'll live beyond a hundred, but I don't think I'll be living for two thousand years!

So the best chance that we have is to get as many people equipped with the *true* gospel to impact and influence as many people as we can in our little lifetime of a hundred to a hundred and twenty years. Do you get that? It's not about us playing.

This is why we're trying to get on TV. This is why we're on the internet. This is why we're pushing and pushing and getting information out there. It's because we have an enormous, *enormous* challenge ahead of us to reach the world for the Kingdom. Amen?

✹ Part Two ✻

As I stated earlier, in part three we will talk about the origin of the gospel and identify when the change took place. In this chapter we are looking at "which gospel." This is part two.

The American Gospel that is preached in the corporate American churches which identify themselves as Christian or as Christianity **did not originate with Yeshua/Jesus.** This may be a surprise to some people, but to some of you it is no surprise at all. It did not originate with Yeshua (or as people refer to him as Jesus).

In fact, **what is preached today in the corporate American Westernized church is very different from the gospel that Yeshua/Jesus preached in his day.** You'll hear me say things like "the *true* Gospel of the Kingdom." What I try to do when making that statement is this. You don't see the Gospel of the Kingdom as far as a sentence in the Bible, but we do see the Gospel of the Kingdom.

We all know that there are those who have preached what they say is the Gospel of the Kingdom, only for us to realize that it wasn't the *true* Gospel of the Kingdom. It was a gospel and it was of a kingdom. Are you hearing me? We have also identified that there are those who have sought to build their own empire. They've sought to build their own ministry. They've sought to build their own name and reputation.

Denominations are the work and result of men. **Denominations didn't originate from the word. They originated with men.** These men who originated these denominations have established hierarchies within those denominations. People are joining denominations under the guise of joining a church.

The gospel that is being exported from America and that is impacting churches and religious life worldwide is a Western version of the gospel that originated with the Hebrew Messiah called Yeshua. The gospel we know today in America has gone through several phases or transitions. That means all versions, however you look at them.

We talked in the first chapter about the Americanized gospel.

1. The Americanized gospel, before it was Americanized, was Westernized.

2. Before it was Westernized, it was Europeanized.

3. Before it was Europeanized, it was Latinized.

I am making these transitions known to people because in the next slide or two you're going to see that the Westernized/Europeanized/Anglo-Saxonized gospels are all similar, but they all have their own individual impact on the gospel as we know it today or the gospel that is being preached today.

4. Before it was Latinized (or Latin), it was Grecized.

5. Before it was Grecized, it was Aramaic and Hebrew.

When we reverse the order, here is the evolution that the gospel has gone through:

1. From Hebrew/Aramaic to Greek

That's a translation, so the gospel that was Hebrew in its origin was translated into Greek. We know that in the translation are words that don't translate. The translator has to figure out the best way to communicate the translation in the language into which it is being translated without losing or getting too far off from the meaning of what they are trying to communicate.

I don't consider this to be "error." I consider it to be individuals who, to the best of their ability, are trying to communicate what is being translated and are staying as close to the translation as they possibly can. That's honorable and that's integrity. **It is dishonorable and not integrity when people insert words that don't belong.**

Look at the effect that this has had on individuals who come under the knowledge or the supposed knowledge of the Messiah.

A good illustration is "Easter." **Easter was actually inserted into the Bible. There is no celebration recognition of Easter in any part of the Scripture other than in one place (in _Acts 12_) where <u>the translators inserted a word that doesn't belong</u>.**

I have to say that even though they inserted a word that doesn't belong, they left the definition of the word that _did_ belong there with it and therefore asserted the definition of the actual word to the word that doesn't belong. But over time it didn't stand because everybody now knows that although "Easter" was used to replace "Passover" [Pesach]; Easter and Passover are two separate, distinct celebrations among the people who follow Messiah. Those who are in the church follow Easter and those who are in Messiah follow Passover.

Then it went:

2. From Greek to Latin

Latin had a great influence on the formulation of the English Bible. That is because the _Latin Vulgate_, which was written from a Latin perspective in translation, was essential in the translation and getting to us what we know of today as the _King James Version_ of the Bible.

3. From Latin to European/Westernized (Anglo-Saxon/Old English)

The thing about the European version (which is why I put Westernized, Anglo-Saxon/Old English) is that the Europeans have a variety of regions of people who speak different languages. The European Union is a compilation of nations that have come together from various parts of Europe and that have different languages, culture, origins, and beliefs.

Then:

4. From European/Westernized (Anglo-Saxon/Old English) to American English

Those of you who have a 1611 King James Bible; if you compare it to a King James Bible of today, you will see that there are *huge* language variations.

Then:

5. From American English to the various translations of Bibles shipped around the world

There are various translations that are now being preached or used in churches around the world.

The Wrong Gospel

When we went to Israel on mission work, I was very surprised. For people who don't get outside of the United States of America; don't think for a moment that everybody in places outside of the United States of America thinks and acts like Americans.

This is why it surprised me. It shocked me to be in Israel in an Israeli church that was worshipping like Americans. They were even using the name "Jesus Christ!" Now, we know that Mary didn't name her baby "Jesus," but that is what the King James says. Now the English translation of the Bible is being translated into other languages, so the customs and culture of the American English Bible are being translated and exported to the various nations around the world.

That's not the gospel that Yeshua told us to take to the nations of the world! Is it any wonder that the end hasn't come yet?

The word "*gospel*" is the English word used to translate the Greek word for "good news." Christians use the word to designate the message and story of God's saving activity through the life, ministry, death, burial, and resurrection of Elohim's unique Son, Yeshua (Jesus).

We aren't going to get into this here. We're going to get into this in the next chapter. We'll see how the gospel that *Yeshua preached* became the gospel *about Yeshua*.

These are two totally different gospels, ladies and gentlemen! These are two totally different gospels, therefore they have two totally different impacts on the peoples' lives that hear these gospels.

Many of us have labored and spent an enormous amount of time in Christian churches, worshiping on Sundays, celebrating Christmas and Easter, and all of the other Christian religious observations, only to find out that **we have been duped!** You know that you were duped! I just came to conclude that I was duped. Then I got angry at the people who duped me, like it was their fault. *They were duped too!* You know, my parents were duped! My grandparents were duped!

The prophet says:

"You know, we inherited lies!"

We inherited a lot of lies. Do you know that the more I walk down this path, the more I realize that there are still some [of these] lies lying dormant in me? They come up at the oddest times. I'll never forget this last Passover. We were talking about horseradish.[2] It was like:

"Where did that come from?"

It was dormant. There are things that are dormant. These are systems, programs that are operating in our heads behind the scenes. They are based on what has been subliminally planted in our spirit over the course of our walk and life.

Our American society has been so infiltrated. It has incorporated a Christian belief system that has led many to say that this nation is a "Christian nation." You are going to see how the Constitution of the United States was impacted not by the Torah, but by the interpretation of Christians when they looked at the Old Testament that they declared was no longer valuable.

---

[2] Arthur had the realization during the Pesach broadcast that his prior recommendation of having horseradish as part of the Passover celebratory meal was a religious teaching and not a biblical one.

Imagine that. At what point in American history did our ancestors, the founders of this nation or the forefathers of this country keep the Sabbath, celebrate the Passover or any of the other [biblical] feasts? Never! So when people say to me:

> *"Well, the Constitution was based on the Torah."*

I say:

> *"Really? You mean that the Constitution was based on the Christian interpretation of the Torah, which they reject."*

Now, don't hate me folks. I'm just a messenger. That's who I am. It's like this. I am dealing with so many different individuals when I deal with this stuff. I get these letters all of the time. I get a lot of stuff that I don't share because to me it isn't even worth sharing, but it identifies where people are. I'm getting letters that the "true" Hebrews are all Black and that White people "have leprosy."

When you see these people who are standing on corners and cussing people out and calling people "White devils" and all of these kinds of things, it is based on a doctrine, folks. That is based on a doctrine where individuals who were duped got some revelation and started reading some books. They went all the way over yonder in rejecting this book [Bible] that they say is the "White man's religion."

The things that we have been taught have impacted our society. They have impacted and formulated religious beliefs and systems. A lot of this rejection of what you teach is based on the falsity of what has been taught; therefore you and I are being put into categories. We have separated ourselves from the categories that people are trying to put us in, but what we still have resembles some of the things that we have separated ourselves from.

I remember personally (as they say) "throwing out the baby with the bathwater." No matter what people say about this book, [Bible] I truly believe that this book contains the truth of

YeHoVaH, our Elohim. There's no doubt whatsoever in my mind that this book contains YeHoVaH's truth. But I also have to say that there's no doubt in my mind whatsoever that there are some manmade effects and traditions that have also been incorporated into this book.

As a student, follower, and disciple of Messiah, I have to (and you have to) be able to distinguish between the religions and traditions of men from the word of YeHoVaH. If you don't, you'll be practicing religion and traditions thinking that you are walking in the truth, when the truth is mixed. There's a mixture. We have to get the mixture out if we're going to fully walk in the authority and power that this word is designed to cause us to walk in.

I'm willing to take the shots. I'm willing to take the missiles. I'm willing to take the arrows; whatever is necessary. I was thinking this morning. This is just me letting you into my head. I believe that what Father is doing in the midst of this ministry and the things that we are teaching is going to revolutionize this world, but it may be a few months or a few years out.

The things that we are laying out, the doctrines that we are laying out and the teachings that we are laying out and recording and putting into books and DVDs are going to have a profound impact on future generations. A lot of the things that are going on right now and the things that are being taught right now ladies and gentlemen, some of you will get, but this is not just for you. This is for our children and our childrens' children and our childrens' childrens' children, if Messiah tarries.

Imagine if we had this when we were children! No, we didn't have it. We had a whole lot of other stuff and we waddled through and were dragged through that other stuff. We brought a lot of that other stuff with us. Then we realized that a lot of the stuff that we had was empty. This is why we now see that:

> *"Hey. I see now why I didn't grow. I <u>knew</u> there was something missing. I just couldn't put my finger on it."*

We're helping people put their fingers on it, so what I have to go through and deal with is nothing. I am not backing down! Halleluyah!

Although "*gospel*" translates a Greek word from the New Testament, the concept of "good news" itself finds its roots in the Hebrew language of the Old Testament.

Merriam Webster defines "*gospel*" as **1a:** the message concerning Christ, the Kingdom of God and salvation. People who don't have biblical tools go to Merriam Webster. That's where they are getting their understanding from. Why? That's because they are reading English words. You don't go to a Greek dictionary to find out the definition of an English word. You go to what? An English dictionary.

People are going to *Merriam Webster* and *Encyclopedia Britannica* to do their study in the Scriptures! **That's not the right place to be looking!**

Another definition [from Webster's] is **1b:** one of the first four New Testament books telling of the life, death, and resurrection of Jesus Christ, also **1c:** an interpretation of the Christian message *the social gospel.*

Then **2:** a lection, which is a liturgical reading from one of the New Testament gospels.

If you haven't been in a Lutheran or an Episcopal or a Catholic Church, you have no idea what a liturgical reading is. You may have heard of "liturgical dancing," but when it comes down to a liturgical reading, this is something that is deep in the tradition of some denominations. They say that you haven't had "church" unless you have had "the liturgy."

Other Webster's definitions are **3:** the message or teachings of a religious teacher; **4:** something accepted or promoted as infallible truth or as a guiding principle or doctrine. That's Merriam Webster.

I'm going to share with you at the end of this chapter when leading into the next chapter, the actual definition and where the word "gospel" came from.

We're going to trace the origin and then we're going to see where it literally changed to what it is today and where the beginning happened. We are going to see all of that.

The gospel that Yeshua taught and the gospel his disciples taught is not the same gospel that is being taught in the Westernized church today. The gospel that is preached in America today has been Westernized and Christianized **and therefore has taken on a totally new identity.**

It is highly possible that the gospel preached today in America is the other gospel that the Apostle Paul referenced in his writing. Now, I can't say that definitively, but I can say definitively that the gospel that is being preached in America today is not the same gospel that Yeshua and his disciples preached and I can show you that, which I am. We will discuss this later in this teaching.

When we hear the word "gospel" in America today, several biblical references come to mind. We can see that just from Merriam Webster because Merriam Webster gave us five different definitions of the gospel. In one, he gave us three distinct definitions in relation to the first definition he gave. Then he gave us four more.

You have all of these different definitions, so when people hear "gospel," people are hearing different things. You are saying one thing and they are hearing something else. They are saying one thing and you are hearing something else. You always seem to be on this link that doesn't seem to connect until you define what you mean and then move on from there.

Here are some of the things that you are going to see in the Bible and which seemingly feed some of the confusion. This is why we must search the Scriptures.

- The Gospel of YeHoVaH/Elohim/God
- The Gospel of Yeshua/Jesus

- The Gospel of the Kingdom of Elohim/God

You are going to find all of these references to the gospel in the book.

- The Synoptic Gospels

It's not in the book, but it is in theology.

- Paul's Gospel

Yes, there is Paul's Gospel.

- The Other Gospel
- The Everlasting Gospel

And then:

- The Gospel of *Revelation*

Most people don't see *Revelation* as a Gospel, but I'll tell you that *Revelation* is probably the only *true* gospel. Why? Because it came from YeHoVaH and was given by Yeshua. Yeah. We're going to see that.

- The Gospel of YeHoVaH/Elohim/God

Romans 1:1 – "Paul, a servant of Yeshua Messiah, called to be an apostle, separated unto…"

What?

"…the gospel of God."

This is what Paul wrote, so one would have to ask:

"Is the Gospel of God, the Gospel of Jesus, the Gospel of the Kingdom – are they the same?"

In essence, what we see and what we find is that it is the same. So if it is the same, why use all of these different terms? Why can't we just say "the Gospel of the Kingdom?" It's because that is not how it is written. Therefore when it is written, it indicates that it is something else, which creates layers of conversations that have to be unlayered [dismantled].

That's unfortunate because a lot of the conversation that takes place is in "unlayering" stuff. If one person or two or three people (or whatever) all took part and developed a pattern in how things were going to be developed in the Scriptures and which books were going to be included in it, then we would have the same or a similar language.

But you also have to understand that if the era of *Job* wasn't an era where the language was a specific language, then in *Job,* the words are going to be from that language. We know that *Job* was probably the first book written.

When Moses comes along, Moses has a variety of languages. We see that Moses learned in the Egyptian's home. He was raised by a Hebrew girl, his sister. He was able to communicate with the various people of the kingdom of Egypt; even with Midian. We see a span where Moses went from Egypt to Midian and there's no indication that the language of the people changed.

There was a change in language, but we don't see Moses riding around with a translator. The assumption is that Moses spoke all of the different languages of the people that he encountered. When we read the English Bible, we are reading a book that is in one language and that incorporates people who didn't speak the same language. There is no indication that there was a different language. So from the perspective of an American reading the Bible, they would assume from *Genesis* to *Revelation* that everybody spoke English.

You see, people become really simple-minded when it comes to the Bible, but when it comes to other things, they get technical. Yeah, they get really technical. They want to "split hairs" on you. They "swallow camels" and "strain at gnats."

- The Gospel of Yeshua/Jesus

Mark 1:1 – "The beginning of the gospel of Yeshua Messiah, the Son of Elohim;"

Before there was the gospel that was written, there was the gospel that was spoken. Now, Yeshua comes onto the scene and speaks. He is preaching the gospel. Twenty-five or thirty years later there is a recording. Do you hear what I'm saying here? The first recorded idea of the first book of the Bible didn't occur until (at the earliest) 55 AD. That's what? Twenty years after Yeshua was sitting in Heaven. Now, imagine if we took twenty years to get our recording out.

I was part of churches where they said:

> *"Listen guys. We've got to get some equipment. We've got to invest in the equipment so that people can have the recording of the teaching before they leave the building."*

So the cassette tapes were enabled. Man, they were doing some editing and giving raw forms. A person could have a cassette tape of the service before they left. They had to wait a little bit, but they had them! Then [the technology] got to the CD and they had the CD before they left! Of course these were unedited, but it was so (how would I put it?) orchestrated in such a way that it was like – what do they call it when you have a dance or something? It was choreographed.

Services are so choreographed and the preaching is so point-driven to the point where while the preacher is preaching the teaching, he's thinking about the CDs and the DVDs.

> *"We've got to get this just right to get the proper recording into the peoples' hands because we don't have time to edit. So we've got to stay on point, and if it's twenty minutes…"*

Most of you don't realize that a lot of preachers are practicing in their studies or their rectories.

> *"Okay, that took me twenty-five minutes. I have to shave five minutes off of this sermon."*

You see, you all don't see this stuff. I mean, think about it. A preacher has twenty minutes or (at the most) thirty minutes. If they have two services that are an hour and a half, it is like:

"You don't have time to be led by the Spirit. You better stay on point, pastor. That's because the next group is getting ready to come in, which means that we have to get these people out of here."

That's church! It's just like a slaughterhouse. You just lead them in and lead them out! You go in with your wool on and you come out sheared. Fleeced? [Laughter]

"And next week, we get to do it all over again! Halleluyah! Praise the Lord!"

This is where people are talking about how:

"You need to stay on point!"

Why? Because that's how you have been trained.

"Why do you keep going on rabbit trails?"

Well, I call them rabbit trails, but let me stop calling them rabbit trails. Let me call them **Spirit-led trails.**

"Well, it just adds so much time in the teaching."

Well, where are you going?

"Preacher!:

[Arthur holds up his arm and points to his watch.] Listen. You aren't in one of those churches where they used to have three and four services and you go to the early one so you can have the rest of your day [to yourself]. We aren't in that place! [Laughter] Halleluyah.

What Yeshua taught (spoke) is the gospel that Yeshua preached. The gospel that Yeshua preached is the Gospel of Yeshua (a/k/a Jesus) or the Gospel of Messiah (a/k/a Jesus Christ).

There are some people who, no matter how many times you tell them that his Momma named him "Yeshua," will say:

"Well, I know him as 'Jesus.' There's no name like the name 'Jesus' and he'll always be 'Jesus' to me!"

[Laughter]

Okay. Now I know that I'm dealing with a thickheaded person. That's it. What you're telling me is that you aren't open for truth.

"I just figured out [tapping watch] that it's time to go."

Halleluyah.

The Gospel of the Kingdom

- There is the Gospel of the Kingdom of God

This is what it says in *Mark 1:14-15*. Please pay attention here.

Mark 1:14-15 – "Now after that John was put in prison, Yeshua came into Galilee, preaching the gospel of the kingdom of God,"

Or Elohim.

[15] *"And saying, 'The time is fulfilled, and the kingdom of God is at hand: repent ye, and believe the gospel.'"*

That's what he said. For those of you who like nutshells, this is the gospel in a nutshell.

"Repent."

Repent from what?

"Repent and believe the gospel."

"Well, what's the gospel?"

Yeshua! Yeshua is the gospel! He wasn't talking about some death, burial, resurrection and ascension! That's part of solidifying your faith. Here's the deal. Paul puts it this way. If he didn't resurrect, our faith is in vain. But Yeshua didn't come preaching about his death, burial and resurrection. As a matter of fact, he preached for months before he even brought up the subject of death.

So what was he preaching about all of that time?

Do you know what else? AFTER his resurrection, he came back! **For forty days he was preaching the things pertaining to the Kingdom.** This is AFTER the death, burial and resurrection. He was preaching the stuff that he was preaching before the death, burial and resurrection.

The written gospels are what we refer to [sic] toady. [There is an error on the PowerPoint slide that needs correcting.] No, that's "today." [Laughter] How did "toady" get in there? There are people who would say:

> *"You know, the toad...there it is! He just made a slip! That's that devil!"*

You know, I was in a church that said that frogs were demonic spirits!

> *"He's got that 'frog' spirit!"*

So let me make sure that I change that before I get an email saying:

> *"See there?!"*

Halleluyah!

The written gospels are what we refer to today as:

- The Gospel of *Matthew*
- The Gospel of *Mark*
- The Gospel of *Luke*
- The Gospel of *John*

Then we talked about the Synoptic Gospels. The gospels of *Matthew, Mark* and *Luke* are referred to as the **Synoptic Gospels** because they include many of the same stories; often in a similar sequence and in similar wording.

They stand in contrast to *John,* whose content is comparatively distinct. *John's* writings are very distinct from *Matthew, Mark* and *Luke.* You will find a lot of the stories in *Matthew, Mark* and *Luke* that you don't find in *John.* When it comes down to the Synoptic Gospels, you can see how it relates to the dating. This is a little chart (on the next page) that we showed you in the last chapter a little ahead of time because I mentioned the Synoptic Gospels.

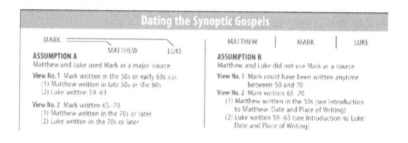

It is believed that *Matthew* and *Luke* used *Mark* as a major source. So as theologians are sitting back and trying to compare things, you have to understand something, folks. **This book [Bible] wasn't handed down from Heaven. YeHoVaH didn't write it and just drop it so Joseph Smith**[3] **could find it.** Some of you all will get that next week. [Arthur is joking.] [Laughter]

Nobody was out in the field and found the King James Version of the Bible. It didn't happen like that. So when we look at how we got it, you will find that there are many books in this book that are in there, but there are a whole lot of them that aren't in there. You'll also find that there were some in here that are no longer in here.

---

[3] Joseph Smith was an American religious leader and alleged prophet and founder of *The Church of Jesus Christ of Latter-day Saints* (Mormons), a manmade religion. He claimed to receive revelation and texts from an angel.

If you've been in this walk for over a year, you've probably run across people who want to get you to read books that are not in the book, as though they should be in the book. Now they're using those books to find new things to try to get you to understand that what you believe is not fully [true].

This book didn't drop from Heaven, nor was it handed from Heaven. It took individuals scouring through many hundreds of writings to determine whether or not it was inspired by the Almighty and deserves to be in the book. But when you are raised up saying:

> *"This is my Bible. This is the infallible, unadulterated word of God and I believe it from Genesis to Revelation or from Genesis to maps..."*

That is unadulterated, infallible; and I say, do you know what? I can buy that. There are some things in there that are unadulterated. There are some things in there that are infallible, but **there are some things in there that aren't.** As a student I have to search.

People don't mind. There are some people who don't want to go to college because they feel:

> *"I don't need to go to college. I didn't even like High School."*

As far as education and knowledge and all of that kind of stuff is concerned, they think:

> *"I've got enough."*

For those people, that's fine, because you don't need to go to college to be successful. You don't need to go to college to be wealthy (if that's what you are seeking). Then there are people who go to college. Anybody who has gone to college and who goes through the book knows that what separates the people who get the "Ds" from the people who get the "As" and the people who are at the top of their class, is their retention. This is where the tests come in.

So a person goes to school. They take the tests. They study so that when the time comes to take the test, they pass. Some people aren't satisfied with a "D" or getting by with a "D" minus. That is barely scraping by. They are not happy with a "C" or a "B." They get an "A" and it's okay, but they'd rather have an "A" plus. There are "A" plus people out there. There are people who won't settle for a low "A." They want their "A" to be at the top of the "A" game. Do you understand what I'm saying?

These are individuals who are meticulous in their study. I will tell you that if you are meticulous in your study like that, that same meticulousness should be applied to the Book of Life. Do you understand? I also find that individuals who went through school casually sometimes go through the Bible casually. It's like, okay. You have the book and when it comes down to going through the classes, now a test is coming. What do you do? You cram!

> *"I need to know this information to pass the test."*

You can translate [or transfer] that to when a person is going through a crisis. They are cramming. They are cramming for verses of Scripture to help them get through that crisis. You should already be "loaded."

If you study, if you search, if you read and if you spend the time; when the crisis comes, you already know how to deal with it. That's because you've already gone through. You're not searching and running all over the place trying to figure stuff out. You're being prepared.

A believer knows that you are either coming out of a crisis, you are in a crisis or you are about to go through a crisis. *Our faith is crisis driven.* You might as well get used to it, because **persecution is crisis.** We're being persecuted on all sides. If you're not being persecuted, you're probably on the wrong side. **You can't walk this walk without persecution!**

So we see that *Mark* and *Luke* here say that they were written in the 50s or early 60s AD (for those of you who are looking). That's the 50s or early 60s.

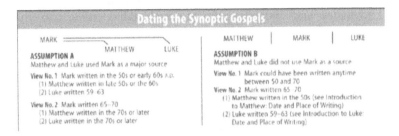

Then over to the right [side of the chart], *Mark* could have been written at any time between 50 and 70 AD.

When it comes down to trying to identify and pinpoint a date when the book was actually written, we know that it wasn't before 50 AD, and we know that Yeshua was around [age] thirty. When he was crucified, he was between thirty-one and a half, thirty-two or thirty-three years old, so 33 AD to 50 AD is how many years?

You've got the teaching and then the "CD" seventeen years later – from memory. Do you get this?

The brothers and sisters in the day of Yeshua were teaching the day after he was crucified. Well, the day after he was resurrected and he found them (or the women), but he was certainly teaching them forty days after his crucifixion.

From ten days after his ascension, we can identify that they began teaching; which was around 33 AD (at the latest). They were teaching, but they weren't teaching per sea from *Matthew, Mark, Luke* and *John.* They were teaching what the gospel taught them to teach.

> *"The things that I taught you are what you are to teach."*

But what is being preached and taught now is what denominations and religions have taught. This is where people get into arguments because **people aren't arguing Scripture,** ladies and gentlemen. **They are arguing doctrine.** Most people don't want to deal with you and the Scriptures. That's because if you have the ability to research, study, point out and have some knowledge and understanding of Greek and Hebrew and you want to meticulously show a person that, they will likely say:

> *"I ain't got time for that. That ain't what I believe."*

So what do you do? How do you show a person if they don't want to hear or have the time to be shown? They keep what they have *concluded* from their "research" (which is really internet perusal).

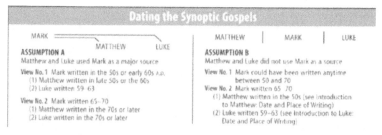

View No. 2: *Mark* was written between 65 and 70 AD. Here it says in **View No. 1** that *Mark* was written between 50 and the early 60s AD. In another assumption (Assumption B), it was written between 50 and 70 AD or between 65 and 70 AD. So we've got a twenty year span here of when *Mark* could possibly have been written. This is based on the theologians who have searched and figured out the possible timelines. They were looking at:

> *"Okay, did he include this? Well, this had happened and this was a very significant event; which means that if he wrote it after this event, this event should have been included in the writing."*

Next there is:

- Paul's Gospel

Paul said in *Romans 2:*

> *Romans 2:12 – "For as many as have sinned without law shall also perish without law: and as many as have sinned in the law shall be judged by the law;"*

Then he says this:

> *Romans 2:13 – "(For not the hearers of the law are just before God, but the doers of the law shall be justified."*

Hmm. That's interesting. **Justification is in doing, not just in hearing.** That's just what *James* says – he who is a hearer of the word. Remember when James wrote his gospel, *Matthew, Mark, Luke* and *John* had not even been written or had been written but was not in full circulation.

You see, when the Gospel of *Mark* was written (who was, by the way, not a follower of Messiah); you don't see the name "Mark" in the twelve disciples. It's not there, so how does Mark get to write a gospel and he wasn't a disciple of Yeshua? Most Christians don't even bother with that. They think that because Mark wrote a gospel, that Mark was one of the disciples. Well, go check out the list! The names are there. They are prominently written. **Mark is nowhere on any of the lists.**

Well, where did Mark get his gospel from if he wasn't a follower of Messiah? That's a good question, yet his gospel was the first one written. Based on the Synoptic Gospels chart, it suggests that these guys (Matthew and Luke) copied from Mark.

Why would Matthew (who followed Messiah) be copying from Mark (who didn't follow Messiah) while Luke was nowhere in the picture? **Notice that you won't find Mark's or Luke's names on the list of the disciples of Yeshua.** Yet Mark and Luke have prominent gospel writings that are relied upon to tell us what Yeshua said; when the fact is that **they got their information from somebody else.**

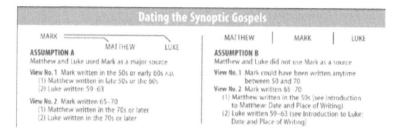

Now they are saying that Matthew and Luke copied Mark! You may say:

> *"Well, what does that have to do with us? Why don't you just preach a good sermon and let's get happy? Let's dance. Bring David in. Do the benediction. Let's eat and fellowship!"*

Because it isn't that kind of party! You see, my goal is to stamp out illiteracy and to drive ignorance out. Those who don't care will be driven out with it. It's not like I'm trying to drive anybody out, but I feel that *we have a responsibility to see what is written and how it was written if we ever expect to live out our faith the way it was intended.*

The Other Gospel

In Paul's gospel, he says:

> *Romans 2:12 – "For as many as have sinned with law..."*

We read that. Verse 14 says:

> *Romans 2:14 – "For when the Gentiles, which have not the law,"*

> *"...when the Gentiles, which have not the law, do by nature the things contained in the law,"*

What do you mean "by nature?" How are they doing "by nature" the things that are contained in the Law? You see, Paul writes some stuff. He says in another place, in *1 Corinthians* chapter *11:*

"Doesn't nature teach that it's a shame for a man to have long hair?"

But:

"Where does nature teach that?"

So it is like:

"Okay Paul. You say some good stuff. I see why Peter wrote what he wrote."

Some people have a hard time sometimes, trying to understand what Paul is writing. I want to understand. But there are people who put Paul over Yeshua, whose teachings were a lot simpler! Are you hearing me?

Romans 2:14 – "For when the Gentiles, which have not the law, do by nature the things contained in the law, these, having not the law, are a law unto themselves:"

Romans 2:15 – "Which show the work of the law written..."

Father is not writing some other writings on the hearts of men. He's writing his Law. The Gentiles which have not the Law, by nature are doing the things contained in the Law. It is like:

"How do they know the Law if they don't have the Law, yet they are doing the Law?"

Well, it shows...

Romans 2:15 – "...the work of the law written in their hearts, their conscience also bearing witness, and their thoughts the mean while accusing or else excusing one another;)"

In other words, the Holy Spirit is using the Law in its conviction of sin. That's the work of the Holy Spirit. It's to convict the world of sin. **Without the Law, there is no sin.** So the Holy Spirit is convicting the hearts of men in accordance to the Law, which they violated.

> Romans 2:16 – *"In the day when God shall judge the secrets of men by Yeshua Messiah according to..."*

What?

> *"...**my gospel.**"*

That's what Paul said. He says:

> *"This is the gospel that I'm preaching. This is my gospel and my gospel is based on what Yeshua did and what Yeshua preached and what he revealed to me."*

> Romans 16:25 – *"Now to him that is of power to stablish you according to..."*

What?

> *"...**my gospel,** and the preaching of Yeshua Messiah, according to the revelation of the mystery, which was kept secret since the world began,"*

Now, there are two individuals in the Bible in the New Testament that received by revelation, directly from Yeshua. One was Paul. Paul wasn't a follower of Messiah, but he received by revelation. Then John, on the Isle of Patmos, received by revelation, the Book of *Revelation*. That is why it is called *Revelation*.

He got a revelation while on Patmos, direct from Messiah and was instructed in the revelation that he received. Yeshua wasn't physically on Patmos, but Yeshua was on Patmos talking to him spiritually. John was writing it down and sending letters from his prison cell.

It is as if he hears way over there on the Isle of Patmos, while totally alienated from all of these congregations yet knowing exactly what was going on in them.

> Romans 16:26 – *"But now is made manifest, and by the scriptures of the prophets, according*

64

*to the commandment of the everlasting Elohim,
made known to all nations for the obedience of
faith:"*

This is *Romans 16* verses 25 and 26. There is:

- Other or another gospel

*2 Corinthians 11:4 – "For if he that cometh
preacheth another Yeshua..."*

There were those – Yeshua even said:

*"Listen. There are some people who are going
to come after me and they are going to say: 'The
Messiah is over there. Yeshua is over there.'"*

He says:

"Don't go!"

But there are going to be some people who go, because they
don't know any better.

"Hey, the Messiah is over there!"

Yeshua warned them. Paul warned them. Peter warned them.

*2 Corinthians 11:4 – "For if he that cometh
preacheth another Yeshua whom we have not
preached..."*

How are you going to know *that* Yeshua from the Yeshua
we're preaching? Well, you listen to what we're preaching and
listen to what they're preaching. Now it's obvious. Can I say this
boldly? **It is obvious that my gospel and some of the
televangelist gospels are not the same gospel.** Isn't that
obvious?

You can turn on Christian TV all day long and you won't
hear this stuff that I'm preaching. As a matter of fact, I watch
these guys "all day long." Well, I don't watch them all day long;
but when I turn them on, they are saying some of the same stuff
[that is different].

> *"Well you know, we're not under the Law.*
> *We're not under the Law. We're under grace.*
> *We're under grace. We're under grace. We're*
> *under grace. Grace, grace, grace, grace! No*
> *Law brother. No Law. No Law. No Law. To be*
> *under the Law is to reject grace."*

Whew! This is why we constantly run into individuals who reject the Law. It's because they are listening to that **other gospel.** Now, *to them,* that other gospel is the "true" gospel. But that other gospel which they call the "true" gospel is opposed to the gospel we are preaching, **so one of our gospels isn't true.** It will always be that way, so here's the option.

You either deny what you believe is the *true* gospel to embrace a gospel you don't believe is true, or they have to deny the gospel that they believe is true to embrace the gospel you are teaching as true. Do you see where the problem is? You've got an impasse. You've got a butting of the heads and a meeting of the minds which won't meet. You've got this gulf. You have to figure out:

> *"Well, how do I get along with people who*
> *reject what I believe to be true?"*

They are everywhere! They are all around us. They're at Grandma's house. They are Grandma! [Laughter] Do you hear what I'm saying? Then you have your children. You want your children to go to Grandma's house, but you know that when your children go to Grandma's house, Grandma is going to try to fill their heads with the stuff that I'm teaching [against]. It is like:

> *"Grandma, how can I bring my children to your*
> *house and you are teaching them stuff that I tell*
> *you I don't believe? I'm not teaching them the*
> *stuff that you're teaching them, Grandma."*

> *"So here's the deal Grandma. Either you stop or*
> *I stop bringing them."*

Now, that's a tough place. How are you going to deny Grandma the children, you know? You have to take the children to see Grandma, but you have to have a supervised visit! You have to supervise the childrens' visit with Grandma. You can't leave them for a split second. We have to deal with that stuff.

Grandma can wear you down! If you think that Mama knows some guilt trips, Mama learned from Grandma! [Laughter] Grandma's the master! You all know I'm telling you the truth. So it creates this problem. Many of us are dealing with some of the problems of our faith.

You see, **your faith is going to cause a problem for you with somebody.** It could be Grandma, Grandpa, Mom, Dad, brothers, sisters or your husband or wife, children (son or daughter), neighbor, friend or coworker. **Your faith is going to cost you.**

Think about this. You work in a company. We live in a society where everybody is taught from early elementary age all the way through the "Ivy League" education to think like a herd [member]. We all flow together. The people who are best at this are the Asians. Asians are good at herd mindsets. This is where communism, socialism and all of that comes in where everybody has to think the same way. Right?

So we're raised in a society of "independent" herd thinking. But when it comes down to the government, everybody has to think "herd," and with the "herd," think about this. You work for a company that has a herd mentality. Now the "herder" says:

> *"We work on Saturday."*

And you say:

> *"Well, master, my faith prohibits me from working on the Sabbath. I love this company. I love my job and I would like for you to make an allowance for me to have the Sabbath off."*

The master may love you. He may like you. He may like you a lot. Now you have just given the master a problem. You see, it would be easier for the master to let you go, but he has all of these other sheep. If he shows favor to you, how is he going to deal with all of them?

Let's say that the master does let you have the Sabbath off. You have to come into a hostile environment. There are people who say:

> *"Who do you think you are, taking the Sabbath off? We have to work on the Sabbath. Why shouldn't you? I don't care about your religion. As a matter of fact, I don't give a !%*@ about your religion!"*

Now you have to deal with these people who have a problem with your faith. Your faith causes you to have a problem. If your faith is not causing you a problem in the world and in the society that you're living in, then you're not living your faith. **That's because your faith is <u>designed</u> to be problematic.** You might as well accept that. Otherwise, go back to the church.

> *"Can't go back there!"*

I know. It says:

> *Galatians 1:6-12 – "I marvel that ye are so soon removed from him that called you into the grace of Messiah unto **another gospel:**"*

Those people who are teaching grace will say that we are under another gospel. That's what they will say. They're not "the ones." We're the ones who have "fallen." We "fell." We "went back under the yoke."

Oh boy. I'm looking forward to the next part of this teaching. It's almost like I want to jump over there right now, but I have to wait. It says:

> *"...**another gospel:**"*
>
> [7] *"Which is not another; but there be some that trouble you, and would **pervert the gospel** of Messiah."*

He talks about the grace of Messiah and the Gospel of Messiah and perverting that gospel.

> [8] *"But though we, or an angel from heaven, preach **any other gospel** unto you than that which we have preached unto you, let him be accursed."*

> [9] *"As we said before, so say I now again, If any man preach **any other gospel** unto you than that ye have received, let him be accursed."*

> [10] *"For do I now persuade men, or God? or do I seek to please men? for if I yet pleased men, I should not be the servant of Messiah."*

What is he saying here? Paul is saying here that the religion that I was in, the faith that I was in was a man-established religion and it was pleasing of men. He says:

> *"Listen. I've changed. I accept Messiah. Before I had the encounter with Messiah, I rejected Messiah and I was welcomed by the men whose gospel I was preaching. But now that I've come into faith in Messiah and have turned away from the gospel of men, I'm no longer preaching the gospel of men. I'm preaching the gospel of Messiah. So I'm not trying to persuade Elohim. It's his gospel that he has given me. If I tried to please men, I would not be a servant of Messiah. I would be their servant."*

He would still be doing what he was doing before he came into the knowledge of faith.

> [11] *"But I certify you, brethren, that **the gospel which was preached of me** is not after man."*

> [12] *"For I neither received it of man, neither was I taught it, but by..."*

Here is where he reveals where he got his gospel. Paul's name is not on the list of followers. **Paul was not a**

disciple/apostle who followed Yeshua. Now we have at least three people in the New Testament whose names were not on the list of Messiah's disciples. We've got Luke and we've got Mark and Paul. **Paul was not a follower of Messiah, so how did he get his gospel?**

He got his gospel by the revelation of Yeshua. In other words, Yeshua visited him. He talks about this in his writings about how he was in the desert for three years, receiving. There were things that he was shown that he couldn't even write about.

Paul was accused of preaching heresy by the religious leaders, however Paul believed the Law and the prophets. You see, the people today who follow Paul; these are the ones who are the "grace" followers. Everybody who wants to follow grace and teach grace; these are some of the things they say. They say that Jesus Christ had to keep the Law in order to "fulfill" the Old Covenant. So once he fulfilled it, he "did away with it." It was "no longer necessary."

We bought that. We believed that, but then it was like:

> *"Okay, how do we live? How do we live our lives if we don't have the Law, the guide book?"*

Well, this is what made the denominations so powerful. If you don't have a guide and a moral standard for how you live your life, then the question now is this:

> *"I'm saved. I gave my life to Jesus Christ, so what do I do?"*

[Then we're told:]

> *"Go to church."*

> *"Okay I'm at church. Now what?"*

> *"Listen to the teaching."*

Okay, I listen. I listen. I spend my life listening and what does that make me? **It made me a member! It made me a Presbyterian! It made me a Methodist! It made me a Catholic! It made me a Baptist! It made me a Pentecostal!**

"Okay. So what about those guys over there that didn't go to your church?"

"Well, they didn't have the truth."

"Well, what's the truth?"

"The truth is what we believe!"

"What do you believe?"

"Well, we believe that you have to be baptized in the name of Jesus, not that 'Father, Son, Holy Ghost' stuff."

"We believe that when you get baptized, you gotta speak in tongues! If you don't speak in tongues, you don't have the Spirit."

"We believe that if you follow Jesus, you're going to go to church seven days a week. And you're certainly going to go to church EVERY Sunday!"

It is like:

"Okay, where do you get that stuff from?"

"That's what they taught me!"

"Where?"

"In church!"

"Church? Why?"

"Because you sent me there and that's what they taught me!"

Right? So when you go to church, they say:

"Turn your Bible..."

They read a verse.

"Turn your Bible..."

They read another verse.

"Turn your Bible…"

"Okay, there's your sermon for today. Come back next week and we're going to do the same thing. Pretty soon we're going to have you so indoctrinated that you are so dependent upon this place and you are so afraid of being cut off from it, excommunicated, not given communion, that it will be to the point where you are going to do what we tell you."

"Those people over there…don't listen to them!"

"Those people over there…have nothing to do with them."

"And if the Jehovah's Witnesses come to your house, act like you're not home!"

Some of you have heard this stuff.

"Oh, and the Seventh-Day Adventists…those people…Heh heh…don't pay attention to what they say. They're trying to earn their salvation. Salvation is free!"

Then they get that "look." You know, they get that little look. [Laughter]

"Salvation is free! Right?!"

[Arthur imitates the person being spoken to who automatically nods their head in agreement.] Oh yeah, they've got you.

The Everlasting Gospel

• The Everlasting Gospel

*Revelation 14:6 – "And I saw another angel fly in the midst of heaven, having the **everlasting** gospel…"*

It's like:

"The Everlasting Gospel? What gospel is that? Is that the Gospel of God, the Gospel of the Kingdom, the Gospel of Jesus Christ, Paul's Gospel?"

"...the everlasting gospel to preach..."

Where is this at?

*"And I saw another angel fly in the midst of heaven, having the **everlasting** gospel to preach unto them that dwell on the earth, and to every nation, and kindred, and tongue, and people,"*

That's *Revelation 14:6*. The word "*everlasting*" in the Greek is "*aionios*." It means: **without beginning and end,** that which always has been and always will be; without beginning; without end, never to cease, everlasting. It's usage is forty-two times as "eternal" and twenty-five times as "everlasting."

That means that the gospel does not have a beginning point and it doesn't have an end point. What does that mean? **The gospel was from the beginning.** It didn't come in the beginning. It was from the beginning because Yeshua, who is the gospel, was before the world was made.

That's the Everlasting Gospel. **This gospel has been preached from the beginning.** It came in at the beginning. This is why the Bible is organized the way that it is.

It's amazing where people start at the beginning in *Genesis,* but they reject the beginning when they get to the middle. It is like Jesus came in the middle of the book and did away with everything that was before him:

"All right y'all. Let's walk from here. Let me show you how to do it. Follow me."

"You mean follow the preacher! How are we going to see you? We can't see you. We have to believe that the preacher is preaching what you preach."

All the preacher has to do is this. This is what happened ladies and gentlemen, when we went to church week after week after week. Some of us got "saved" at least fifteen or twenty times. [Laughter]

> *"All right. Ha ha. Every head bowed, every eye closed. We know that some of y'all backslid since the last week. We know that some of you all just didn't do right...in the sight of God. I HEARD some stories from some people. You hear what I'm saying. And so...thank God for his grace...because he's about to give us another chance. Every eye closed, every head bowed."*

> *"Preacher, I opened my eyes and your eyes ain't closed."*

> *"All right. We're going to have an altar call. Now, I know that some of you all...you gave your life to Jesus...but you just still ain't getting it right. But thank him for his mercy. He's a God of second beginnings, third beginnings...new beginnings. So if you need to come down and get a refresher course, a refresher confession, you're welcome at the altar."*

You've got people trekking to the altar and it is like:

> *"Okay, now what?"*

> *"Go back to your seat. We'll be back here next week to do it all over again!"*

This stuff seems funny, but listen folks. We did that stuff with fervor! We did it with all of the faith we could muster up! Do you remember how many times you came down the aisle and you and your knees were shaking? Your voice was trembling. You were sitting there saying:

"Do I need to go up? Did I need to go up with them last week? I don't need to go up this week. Do I need to go up?"

Then the preacher says:

"Stop resisting the Holy Spirit!"

[Laughter]

"That's my cue. That's a sign from God."

You are passing by some folks and they are saying:

"Man, she's gone up three weeks in a row! There ain't that much sin in the world!"

Folks listen. Those of you who are out there online, I know that some of you are tuning in for the first time and you are saying:

"What kind of..."

Whatever. It's all right to have fun. I mean, you know. The joy of YeHoVaH comes in a variety of ways.

"Well, you're making fun of folks!"

I'm not making fun of folks. I'm making fun of *systems*. These are institutions and systems that people have been brainwashed in. This is what makes it hard for some people to come out of those systems and those institutions. Those institutions and systems are like octopus tentacles.

They've got you over here on your job – Christian. They've got you over here at Grandma's house – Christian. They've got you over here on your bowling team – Christian. They've got you over here in your youth group – Christian. They've got you over here in your men's ministry and your women's ministry and when volunteering during the course of the week. They've got tentacles.

To walk away from that church affects so many different aspects of life. It affects your relationship with your siblings. It affects your relationships with your groups that you are a part of.

It affects your relationships in almost every aspect. As a matter of fact, you chose your dentist because he was a Christian (or your doctor). Most of the people that you chose to do work for you are Christians. What about where you shop?

It is so much a part of our daily life that it is to the point where it doesn't rise to the surface until we think about walking away from church. You see, it's not just about walking away from a false teaching, as much as it is walking away from the life that you know. All of the people or the majority of the people that are in your life are a part of that system that you are talking about walking away from.

That's what holds you on. You know that you should have left that place a long time ago, but…

> *"I just can't do it! I mean, you know…where am I gonna go?"*

And that is true.

The Gospel of Revelation

- Revelation

Revelation 1:1 – "The Revelation of Yeshua Messiah, which Elohim gave unto him…"

Who is the revelation of, ladies and gentlemen? Yeshua. And who gave it? YeHoVaH. So YeHoVaH gave Yeshua the revelation to give to his servants.

> *"…which Elohim gave unto him…"*

To whom? To Yeshua.

> *"…to shew unto his servants…"*

Who? John.

> *"…things which must shortly come to pass; and he sent and signified it by his angel unto his servant John:"*

Here it is that John is out there doing his time on the Isle of Patmos, where he had been sent to prison. Then an angel showed up. Angels have shown up all throughout the Bible, so this shouldn't be a surprise to anybody. An angel shows up and John is in there looking like he is talking to himself, but he's having a conversation either with a visible angel or an invisible angel. We don't know.

But we do know that John gives all of these chapters or letters that he is sending to different people in different cities to different Kehillahs or congregations, warning them. It is like:

> *"Who's John? I don't know any John. How does John know us? How does John know what's going on in here?"*

He wrote to one place and said:

> *"You know, I've got a few things against you all. You've got that woman in there, that Jezebel. Some of you all think you're rich, but you're poor, naked and blind."*

I mean, he's calling them out and John isn't even a member of the church! They can't put him out! I mean, there is something about prison. After awhile, you kind of get bored and it's like:

> *"I've got nothing to lose."*

It's unfortunate that we have to get to that point before we put some "concrete in our heels" and stand for Yeshua. I'm going to say this again. **Your faith is designed to create problems for you in the natural. Your faith is designed to cause conflict with your environment.**

The Gospel of *Revelation* included keeping YeHoVaH's commandments and faith in Yeshua. Whose gospel was it? The *Revelation* is whose revelation? It is the revelation of Messiah Yeshua! It came from YeHoVaH and was given to John! We find out in *Revelation*:

- The Everlasting Gospel

Revelation 14:6 – "And I saw another angel fly in the midst of heaven, having…"

There's a lot of angelic activity going on in *Revelation*. There are angels all over the place giving messages and talking to people. This angel had:

> *"…the **everlasting** gospel to preach unto them that dwell on the earth, and to every nation, and kindred, and tongue, and people,"*

That is to *every* nation and *every* kindred and *every* tongue and *every* people. It's a gospel of revelation! It's the Everlasting Gospel! Even though *Revelation* is at the end of the book, the everlasting is from the beginning. **It's the gospel that always was and shall always be!** It is speaking of things that shall surely come to pass – even though they haven't yet.

This gospel included keeping YeHoVaH's commandments AND faith in Yeshua. **You can't have one without the other. You can't keep the commands and reject Yeshua and you can't love Yeshua and reject the commands!** How do I know? *Revelation 12.*

> *Revelation 12:17 – "And the dragon was wroth with the woman, and went to make war with the remnant of her seed…"*

Who is her seed? The remnant, those:

> *"…which **keep the commandments of Elohim, and** have the testimony of Yeshua Messiah."*

Who's preaching this? YESHUA!

> *Revelation 14:12 – "Here is the patience of the* **saints:***"*

The who? The holy ones! The called-out ones! The set apart ones!

> *"…here are they that…"*

What?

"...keep the commandments of Elohim, <u>and</u> the faith of Yeshua."

Can it get any clearer?

But <u>that's not the gospel that is being preached</u>, ladies and gentlemen! **The gospel that is being preached in the churches today is faith in Jesus and faith only.** There is none of the other stuff.

"We're not under the Law, we're under grace."

"We can't do the Law and be under grace."

It is like:

"Okay, where did <u>that</u> gospel come from?"

It's a made-up gospel that people cut and paste from Paul's writings! You might say:

"Well, how can you prove that the people cut and paste from Paul's writings?"

The Hebrew Roots Gospel

• The Hebrew Roots Gospel

When I talk about Hebrew Roots, I am not talking about a movement or a religion or a denomination. I am talking about the gospel that has its origins in the Hebrew Scriptures. **This Hebrew Roots Gospel is the Everlasting Gospel.**

The Hebrew Roots Gospel <u>is</u> the Everlasting Gospel

When I talk about Hebrew Roots faith, I mean tracing our faith back to its origin. **The origin of our faith is rooted in**

Hebrew. The speakers were Hebrew. The writers (with the exception of Luke) were Hebrew. The language was Hebrew.

Luke is the only non-Hebrew who wrote any book in the New Testament. Luke was Greek. He wasn't Hebrew. This is not something made up, but is a verifiable fact which nobody can deny.

The Hebrew Roots Gospel originated among the Hebrew people. The Book of *Hebrews'* writer spoke of the gospel in his day in both present and past tenses.

> *Hebrews 4:1 – "Let us therefore fear, lest, a promise being left us of entering into his rest, any of you should seem to come short of it."*

> *Hebrews 4:2 – "For <u>unto us</u> was the gospel preached, as well as unto them:"*

The context here is referring to those who were in the wilderness. This gospel was the same gospel.

> *"...but the word preached did not profit them,"*

Why? Because they didn't mix it with faith.

> *"...not being mixed with faith in them that heard it."*

So faith was with them. They heard the Almighty speak, but they didn't believe what the Almighty said. They heard, but they didn't do. Why didn't they do? It was because they didn't believe. Are you with me?

> *Hebrews 4:3 – "For we which have believed do enter into rest, as he said, 'As I have sworn in my wrath, if they shall enter into my rest: although the works were finished from the foundation of the world.'"*

Do you see how he ties this gospel and the rest all the way back to the foundation? Well, it's beyond the beginning, but to the foundation. The foundation came before the actual Earth was laid. Do you see this?

Peter speaks of the gospel being preached to those of old.

> *1 Peter 4:6 – "For this is the reason the gospel was preached even to those who are now dead,"*

It doesn't mean that Yeshua preached to dead people. It is that the people who heard the gospel are now dead.

> *"...so that they might be judged..."*

> *"...so that they might be judged according to men in the spirit."*

Why? The gospel is spiritual.

The gospel came to us today through the Hebrew people, the people of Israel, the descendants of Abraham, whom YeHoVaH made covenant with. Again, although the word "gospel" is not found in the Tanach/Tanakh/Old Testament, the definition or meaning of the word "gospel" as we know it is there.

Abraham was a descendant of Eber, which means "Hebrew." The Hebrew word that best describes or defines the word we know as "gospel" is "**Bisar**." [4] We're going to get to this in the next chapter.

Again, Paul was accused of preaching heresy by the religious leaders; however Paul believed the Law and the prophets. **People get the idea that Paul preached against the Law.** They believe that Paul's teaching on grace was opposed to the Law. Then there are those who say:

> *"Well, Paul kept the Law to win some people who were under the Law."*

Let's say that is true, because Paul said that he became "all things to all people that he might win a few." So the question that one would have is this. If Paul preached the Law that he

---

[4] The spelling of "*Bisar*" is from the *Holman Bible Dictionary*. In other places in this text you will see "*Basar*," which is from the *Strong's Hebrew Dictionary*. Both words have the same meaning and represent the same word.

might win people under the Law, did he believe it or was he doing it to win them? I ask this because of what Paul said about himself.

What the preachers say about Paul is their opinion. You see, what I do is try to find the people they are talking about and see what they say. Here's what Paul said about himself. You will find in the Bible where Paul says that he became all things to all men that he might win a few. Then a person will say:

> *"Paul preached the Law to people who are under the Law, but Paul didn't keep the Law."*

When you show people that they are wrong and all of that, the next angle they take is this:

> *"Well, Paul kept the Law because he was Jewish."*

So now the philosophy behind that is if Paul kept the Law because he was Jewish, then they say:

> *"He was Jewish. I'm not."*

> *"Gentiles don't have to keep the Law. That's for the Jews."*

Do you see how that logic just keeps cycling? The bottom line is that:

> *"You can take your Law-abiding self and get the (you know where) out of here."*

That's what they're saying. It is like you just take your Law and go on (and your grace and your faith and your favor and your money and your blessings and your assets).

You see, the people who reject your Messiah come to you when they need something. They don't want to hear your gospel, but open up that wallet, brother. They don't want to hear your truth because they've got "truth," but their truth doesn't sustain them. They don't want to hear your teaching or your lectures. They just want your help. And if [they] say:

> *"Now, I know you all keep that Law stuff, but if you say that you're a believer in Jesus...Ha ha ha. You're supposed to help me because I asked you...Give to them, whoever asks."*

It is like:

> *"You know, you all just twist stuff. I mean, you're just twisting and twisting and twisting; whatever works to your advantage and favor is how you twist the Scriptures."*

They are just pulling stuff out of everywhere. Then when you try to pinpoint something, it's:

> *"Well, you know..."*

You get them here. Then they want to jump to another Scripture. You get them here. Then they want to jump to another Scripture. Pretty soon they have worn you out jumping all over the place. It's because they're not solid. In here we're trying to get people "solid."

This is what Paul said about himself:

> *Acts 24:14 – "But this I confess unto thee, that after the way which they call heresy, so worship I the God of my fathers,"*

They say I'm a heretic, but I worship my Father:

> *"...believing all things"*

Paul says:

> *"I believe. I'm not just doing this to win some people. I believe all things..."*

> *"...which are written in the law and in the prophets:"*

You see, **Paul practiced these things.** He lived these things. **Yeshua practiced these things.** He lived these things. The disciples and apostles practiced those things and lived those things. Then with the last gospel (*Revelation*); the interesting thing about this gospel is that it is said to have been written between 95 and 100 AD. It is said that this "John" is one of the longest-living persons among the apostles. Of course some say that *this* John may not have been "that" John.

Nevertheless, John received revelation. He preached the gospel from a prison. He received direct revelation from the Almighty through Messiah via an angel. John had his head on straight because with *Revelation,* he is saying:

> *"Listen. The saints are they that have faith in Yeshua, but they also understand the commands of YeHoVaH."*

⭐ **Part Three** ⭐

The Origin and the Change

This next teaching will be on when the Testaments (Old and New) became separated. The separation of the testaments was when the Old Testament began to be looked at in a different light than the New Testament. It was there that the other gospel actually took on its power and authority to become what we know of today as the American Gospel.

For some reason or another, intelligent people – and I say "intelligent," although there is a difference. Being intelligent in Science, Mathematics, English and all of the other educational subjects doesn't necessarily make us intelligent when it comes to the things of the Bible. There is a literacy and a competence level that people obtain and attain in the educational arena, but that doesn't make people biblically literate.

As a matter of fact, I am amazed sometimes. I used to hear an expression when I was a child. It was:

"You don't get old being a fool."

Has anybody ever heard that?

"You don't get old being a fool."

Yet I knew a lot of old fools. A fool says in his heart:

"There is no God."

That's a fool talking right there. There are a lot of old fools. There are a lot of people who are old and who reject the authority of the Creator in their lives. Then there are elderly people in the body of Messiah who are biblically illiterate. Just because a person is of age doesn't necessarily make them wise.

You can be wise in the things of the world. The Bible says that there is a worldly wisdom. That wisdom is Earthly. It is sensual and what? Devilish.

When I see old people trying to act like they aren't old people, it is like someone who is wrestling with the "evolution" that the Almighty has designed. We are young and we get old. When we get old in him, there is a wisdom that is supposed to materialize in our lives as we are growing in him and drawing closer to him.

There are people who are in what is known as the "Christian kingdom." That doesn't necessarily mean that they project from themselves that they are mature in the things of Elohim. That's the only way I can put it. They are mature in their doctrine and in their denomination.

But how many of you know that there are people who are old (elderly) people in one denomination and that have issues with another? I'm hoping that we'll get to a point in this chapter where we'll look at some translations.

The American Gospel that is preached in the corporate American churches which identify as "Christianity" did not originate with Yeshua/Jesus. In fact, what is preached today in the corporate American Westernized church is very different from the gospel that Yeshua/Jesus preached in his day.

The gospel that is being exported from America and that is impacting churches and religious life worldwide is a Western version of the gospel that originated with the Hebrew Messiah called Yeshua. The gospel that we know today in America has gone through several phases or transitions. This is for all of the versions, no matter how you look at them.

Although "gospel" translates a Greek word from the New Testament, the concept of "good news" itself finds its roots in the Hebrew language of the Old Testament. **The gospel that Yeshua taught and the gospel his disciples taught is not the same gospel that is being taught in the Westernized church today.** The gospel that is preached in America today has been Westernized and Christianized and therefore has taken on a totally new identity.

It is highly possible that the gospel that is preached today in America is the "other gospel" that the Apostle Paul referenced in his writing. We are going to discuss this here and we are going to look at some of this.

When I say this, there are some people out there that will automatically get upset with me. You know, when you're teaching the truth and what you believe to be truth, there are other people who have a different "truth" than your truth. You do know that, right? There are people who believe very differently than we do. As a matter of fact, there are people out there who think that we have literally lost our minds.

They believe that we were "once saved" when we believed in Jesus. But when we stopped calling Jesus "Jesus" and started calling Jesus "Yeshua"; and when we stopped going to church on Sunday and started keeping the Sabbath and rejected Christmas and Easter and all of that other pagan tradition that has infiltrated the Christian church and we started keeping the biblical holy days, people said (and think) that we have left salvation.

They believe we have "fallen from grace." They believe we have rejected the teachings of Yeshua. **To reject the teachings of Yeshua is like rejecting Yeshua.** But their idea is that if we don't do what is traditionally and typically done by Christians around the world, that we have denied what Yeshua did on the cross!

There are people who believe of those of you in this room (and many of you who are sitting on screens around America and around the world on the internet) that because you have taken this path, you have denied the redemptive work of Yeshua. They believe that you have rejected the grace that he brought to us and have left the grace and gone back under the Law and fallen from grace and are therefore cursed.

You know that I'm telling you the truth! There are people who think that you are cursed! That's a fact! That's just the way that it is! So for us to continue down this path, it is immediately and automatically going to create some divisions with people that we love and care about. These are people who have chosen to go a different path than the path that we are on.

When I talk about Hebrew Roots faith, I mean tracing our faith back to its origin. **The origin of our faith is rooted in Hebrew.** The speakers were Hebrew. The writers (with the exception of Luke) were Hebrew. The language was Hebrew. This is not something made up, but is a verifiable fact which nobody can deny. The gospel came to us today through the Hebrew people, the people of Israel and descendants of Abraham whom YeHoVaH made covenant with.

The word "gospel" is the English word that is used to translate the Greek word for "good news." This is what most people know the gospel to be. It is the "good news." That's the Greek definition. Preachers today use the word to designate the message and story of YeHoVaH's saving activity through the life, ministry, death and resurrection of Yeshua, the Son of our Elohim (God).

Although "gospel" translates a Greek word from the New Testament, the concept of "good news" itself finds its roots in the Hebrew language of the Old Testament. Here we're going to look at the origin.

Although the word "gospel" is not found in the Tanach/Tanakh/Old Testament, the definition or meaning of the word "gospel" as we know it is there. The Hebrew word that best describes and defines the word we know of as "gospel" is *"Bisar."*

"Bisar" is the Hebrew verb which means "to bear news or to bear tidings." It's not until some time that it becomes "good news." Its origin is to "bear news." It means: news, tidings.

Unlike the English language, Hebrew is able to convey the subject of the proclamation in the verb's root. No direct object was needed with the verb *"bisar"* to make clear that the subject of an announcement was "to bear news" or to "bear tidings."

So originally, the gospel or the word that evolved into what we know of today as the "gospel" was "news." It was "news," "tidings."

Here is the Hebrew for *"Bisar"* [בָּשַׂר]. (*"basar"* {baw-sar'}) It is 01319 in the Strong's numbering. It means: to bear news, bear tidings, publish, preach, show forth; to gladden with good news; to bear news; to announce (salvation) as good news, preach; to receive good news.

These are all of the words that are associated with this particular Hebrew word. Its usage was sixteen times as "tidings," three times as "show forth" and as "publish" and once each as "messenger" and as "preached."

What makes "tidings" to be "good tidings" is when the word "good" is used before it. Are you getting this?

Originally the word *"basar"* was used to deliver news of good tidings; expecting a reward for the tidings. (*2 Samuel 4:10*). You will find this first used there.

Those of you who have gone through our *Discipleship Training Program* know that we talk about the *First Mention Principle*. The First Mention Principle is looking for the time that a word is first used.

Now again, we know that the word "gospel" is not in the Old Testament. You won't find the word "gospel" there, but we're going to show you from the New Testament how it came from the Old Testament. Therefore there are those who think that the gospel originated in the New Testament (when in fact, it did not).

> *2 Samuel 4:10 – "When one told me, saying, 'Behold,'"*

This is David speaking.

> *"'Behold, Saul is dead,' thinking to have brought **good tidings**, I took hold of him, and slew him in Ziklag, who thought that I would have given him a reward for his **tidings**:"*

Those of you who know the situation, know that Saul had an issue with David. Everybody knew that Saul had an issue with David. Now Saul is dead and they expected that David would be happy about that.

You see, we're not to take joy, even when our enemies fall. But there are people who think that when your enemies get what they deserve, that you should rejoice in it. The Torah speaks in opposition to that. We don't rejoice in evil. We don't rejoice in bad and in calamity or in terribleness.

We don't wish "bad" upon our neighbors. As a matter of fact, we're supposed to bless those who curse us! Love those who hate us. Pray for those who despitefully use us. These are easy things to say, but when it comes down to walking it out, that's when the "rubber meets the road."

There are a lot of people who talk about their faith, but when it comes down to walking out their faith, you will come to realize that all they've got is lip service. They honor the Almighty with their lips. I'm going to tell you that **walking out your faith is not easy unless you are totally committed to it!**

There are some things in your flesh. Listen to me please. Your flesh doesn't want to walk out this faith. That's because in order for your flesh to walk out this faith, this flesh has to "die" and your flesh doesn't want to "die." Your flesh is your ego. For many people, their identity is in their flesh, in their natural man.

And don't mess around and get a position [on something]. Do you hear? You'll handle the title, but then you want the pay that goes along with the title. Then when people don't recognize your title, you get upset. Have you ever found that people get upset because you don't recognize their title? It's like:

> "What's your name?"

> "My name is DOC-tuh!" [Doctor]

Really? Have you ever had people say:

> "I'm Doctor..."

Then if you call them by their first name, they've got a problem with it. Or it's:

"Pastor...to you!"

Or:

"Bishop!"

You've never met anybody like that, right? [Arthur laughs] It is like:

"Your identity is in your title?"

Your identity is in the things that go before your name, not your name itself. I have found people who have a real problem with that. Here David is saying:

"Listen. I'm not rejoicing in the fact that Saul, who did not like me and who wanted me dead, is dead."

Saul was a king. The Torah says that *you do not speak ill of your brethren.* You don't do it. But when your brethren do stuff, it makes it easier to speak ill of your brethren. That doesn't excuse you. Do you get this? Just because somebody does something that makes it easier to speak against them doesn't give you the biblical right to do it. Now, you may have the natural, worldly right, but you don't have the scriptural, biblical right to do that.

The phrase "**good tidings**" is from *"basar"* {baw-sar'} meaning: to bear news, bear tidings, publish, preach, show forth. In this particular verse (*2 Samuel 4:10*) you will notice that there are "good tidings" and then there are "tidings," so you have two words here. What separates one from the other is the word "good."

But "good" in and of itself, when associated with "tidings," is not necessarily a word that has a distinct definition from the tidings themself. It's just that the two words become one, which makes them different than "tidings" alone.

We see "good tidings" and "tidings." "Good tidings" is "*basar*" and "tidings" is "*besowrah*" [(0139) {bes-o-raw'}] **These are two different words.**

That's where we see "good news." It means: news, good news, tidings, reward for good news; good tidings, reward for good tidings.[5]

This is when somebody thinks that if they bring you good news that you are going to reward them. *It is distinct from the news itself.* That's how it is used in that verse.

The word "*basar*" was not only used to reference the message, but was once used in reference of the messenger. Here we find:

> 1 Samuel 4:15-17 – "*Now Eli was ninety and eight years old; and his eyes were dim, that he could not see.*"
>
> [16] "*And the man said unto Eli, 'I am he that came out of the army, and I fled to day out of the army.' And he said, 'What is there done, my son?'*"

[He is saying:]

> "*What's happening there? What's going on with my son?*"
>
> [17] "*And the **messenger**...*"

That's the word "*basar*."

> "*...answered and said, 'Israel is fled before the Philistines,'*"

---

[5] The word "*besowrah*" comes from the word "*tidings*" as used in the reference to *2 Samuel 4:10 (KJV)* – "*When one told me, saying, 'Behold, Saul is dead,' thinking to have brought good tidings, I took hold of him, and slew him in Ziklag, who thought that I would have given him a reward for his **tidings**.*"

Is that good news? No! You see, the word "gospel" came from this word and it wasn't good news here! It says:

> *"'...and there hath been also a great slaughter among the people, and thy two sons also, Hophni and Phinehas, are dead'"*

Not only is your son, but your <u>sons</u> (Hophni and Phineas) are dead. Is that good news to Eli? No! This is a messenger of *bad* news, but it is a messenger of news, period. It says:

> *"'...and the ark of Elohim is taken.'"*

There isn't anything good in this verse, but the fact is that **it was the Almighty who was doing it. It was him who was making this happen.** Why? *Because he had warned them.* He had warned Eli about what he was permitting to take place in his family. He had warned him about his children. He had warned him about dealing with them but he refused to hear and obey.

His love for his children was greater than his love for Elohim (so was his love for his family). You see, many of us have been taught that our faith is supposed to pull families together. Now, that may have been the case in Judaism, but when Yeshua came along, he said:

> *"Hold it, hold it hold it, hold it, hold it! That whole scenario has changed. That is not the message. As a matter of fact, the message that I bring is like a sword! It's going to cut! It's going to separate! It's going to divide some stuff!"*

Are you hearing me? Religion might bind people together, but **the gospel has a tendency to divide.** That's just the truth, folks, whether we like that or not.

He says:

> *"Listen. This thing is going to separate a Momma from her daughter; sisters and brothers, nations..."*

Again, that word "messenger" ([01319] "*basar*") is the same word. It means to "bear news." So we see that the messenger can be the messenger and the message.

The word "*bisar*" in a military setting evolved to its use in a personal context. (*Psalms 40:9*).

> *Psalms 40:9 – "I have **preached** righteousness in the great congregation: lo, I have not refrained my lips, O YeHoVaH, thou knowest."*

This word "preached" is what word? "*Basar.*" Again, it means to "bear news," to "bear tidings." We can see under the usage that this word is used sixteen times as "tidings," three times as "show forth," three times as "publish," once as "messenger," once as "**preached**" and it is all the same word!

So far, the word "*basar*" has been used as:

1. Good tidings

2. Messenger

3. Preached

The prophet and writings of *Isaiah* mark the full religious development of the term "*basar*" in the Old Testament. By the time of *Isaiah*, the word "*basar*" was most often used to describe the anticipated deliverance and salvation which would come from the hand of YeHoVaH when the long-awaited Messiah came to deliver Israel.

By the time that Yeshua comes onto the scene, this word has gone through a major evolution. **It has become something other than what it was originally from.**

The prophet says:

> *Isaiah 52:7 – "How beautiful upon the mountains are the feet of him that bringeth **good tidings**, that publisheth peace; that bringeth **good tidings** of good,"*

That word "*basar*" is tidings, news of good, good news.

"...that publisheth <u>salvation</u>; that saith..."

That word "salvation" there is **Yeshua**.

"...that saith unto Zion, 'Thy Elohim reigneth!'"

"How beautiful are the feet of him that brings good tidings; that publish peace, that bringeth good tidings of good that publish Yeshua...that declare, that publish, that proclaim Yeshua, salvation."

The "good tidings" there is the word "*basar.*"

The usage of the New Testament word "gospel" finds its origin in the Old Testament passage of *Isaiah.* Here is how we know. Let's look at the passage.

Isaiah 61:1 – "The Spirit of YeHoVaH Elohim..."

Or the Spirit of Elohim, the LORD...

"...is upon me; because YeHoVaH hath anointed me to..."

To do what?

*"...preach **good tidings** unto the meek;"*

Which is the poor.

"...he hath sent me to bind up the brokenhearted, to proclaim liberty to the captives, and the opening of the prison to them that are bound;"

Please hear this, folks. Even without *Matthew, Mark, Luke* or *John,* every Hebrew who heard this knew that this was speaking about Mashiach (Messiah). They knew that this was speaking about an individual who was coming from the Almighty; so every Hebrew who heard this passage proclaimed knew that it was speaking of Yeshua, who was to come.

That's without the New Testament!

That word "good tidings" (again) is "*basar.*"

The writer Luke, who is a Greek writer, quotes from the Hebrew *Isaiah*, a direct quote where we see the Hebrew word used in a Greek term. When *Luke* quotes from *Isaiah,* the translators take the words "good tidings" and put [replace it with] "*gospel.*" This is what happened! Luke is not writing a passage on his own. He is quoting from that which is already written. Let's see how he does it.

> *Luke 4:18 – "The Spirit of the Lord is upon me, because he hath anointed me to preach the **gospel***"

Do you see this? Now, if Luke was writing from the actual [writing], he would say:

> *"...he has anointed me to preach the **good news.**"*

But no, he puts the word "*gospel.*" So it has **evolved** from the Hebrew "good tidings" to what we know of as the English word "*gospel.*" The word "gospel" isn't even a Greek word. "Gospel" is an English word *that came from* Old English *that came from* Latin *that came from* Greek *that came from* the Hebrew "good tidings." What I have done here is put them side by side to compare them so you can see this.

> *Isaiah 61:1 – "The Spirit of the Lord Elohim is upon me; because YeHoVaH hath anointed me to preach **good tidings** unto the meek;"*

Luke says:

> *Luke 4:18 – "The Spirit of the Lord is upon me, because he hath anointed me to preach the **gospel** to the poor;"*

For the word "poor" there; if you look up the word "meek" in the Hebrew, guess what it is? It is "poor." So when you get the New Testament writings where it changes the words, it has gone through a translation process in order to get to us in its English form.

But because we read it in its English form; even though we see it in its Hebrew origin, in our minds (subconsciously) we make a distinction between the two as if they're two different things. You may say:

"Well, what difference does it make, brother?"

It makes a lot of difference because of the way we are taught to think and how we operate and walk out that thinking in our daily life. It makes a difference even to what we begin to declare and publish with our own mouths.

What we proclaim (based on what we've been taught) is what *we've been taught* versus *what was taught*. I'm not talking about what was taught by our denomination. I am talking about *what was originally taught in the Scriptures*.

Regarding development in the New Testament from approximately 300 BC until after the time of Messiah; Greek was the dominant language of the biblical world. The Greek language crossed geographic and cultural barriers to provide a common tongue for government and for commerce, much like English today.

For most people, English is a second language. English is the predominant language here in the United States. But when it comes down to around the world, guess what is the number one language that is being learned by people who don't speak English? English is the language of commerce. English is the [number one] language.

People would much rather have currency with a dead President than currency with a Queen. The Queen has currency. Her picture is on some currencies like in Britain on the Pound Sterling [£] and all of that. It's a little bit more. I tell you that there is no currency that spends around the world like American currency. The one hundred dollar bill is the most coveted piece of paper on the planet.

If you've not been outside of the United States of America, then you might not realize this. But if you've got hundred dollar bills in your pocket and you go out to some of these other countries, man, you've got power! Interestingly enough, you can spend a one hundred dollar bill practically anywhere in the world. An American one hundred dollar bill (or an American dollar) is the most widely spent currency around the world.

If you bring some of those other currencies to other countries, they won't take them. They won't take them! They will sell you some currencies, but they won't buy them back. It's like:

> *"Nah, we want the dollar, brother!"*

Sure enough, America has influenced the world like no other culture, and guess what? America is one of the youngest countries in the world. Don't quote me on this, but I know that since America was established as a country and as a nation, two other countries could be younger. They are Israel and South Sudan.

I believe that South Sudan is the youngest country. Israel is a little older. America is what, about five hundred years old as far as we understand it? Of course, America was here before it was called "America," but it was not [officially] recognized [as America].

During the same time period, thousands of Israelites emigrated from Palestine throughout Asia Minor. Some people don't like the fact that you can call Israel "Palestine," but before Israel became Israel, it was known by the world as Palestine. Some people say:

> *"Well, you know. The Palestinians are created people."*

And I say:

> *"Well, you know, the Palestinians are people who lived in Palestine."*

That's just a fact, folks. That's not trying to be semantically difficult. It is just speaking what is there.

So there are Israelites (Hebrew people) who moved out of the land before there were persecutions. There were people who moved into the land after the persecutions. Even after YeHoVaH delivered the people from Babylon and they went back into the land, a whole lot of folks didn't go back. A small group of individuals went back.

Even today there are millions of Jews and Hebrews around the world that have no interest whatsoever in going to Israel. It's amazing to me that the people who want to go to Israel the most are Christians and Messianics.

It was really something when we were there. When it came to the feasts, there were Jews who were trying to get out of Israel like you wouldn't believe! It was like:

"Who leaves Israel during the feasts?"

But you see folks, we have been taught to fall in love with an ideology. When we begin to look at the facts, sometimes people get upset with the fact presenter. Therefore the messenger gets attacked so that the message can be delineated or diminished or rejected.

During this time, many devout Greek-speaking Israelites lived in the lands surrounding the Mediterranean Sea. In fact, many who lived outside of Palestine spoke Greek better than they spoke Hebrew. Eventually they translated their Scriptures and the important expressions of their faith into the Greek *Septuagint* (sometimes abbreviated LXX). This is the name that was given to the Greek translation of the Hebrew Scriptures. The Septuagint has its origin in Alexandria, Egypt and was translated between 300-200 BC.

We see this issue taking place in *Acts* where the deacons are established because of a dispute between the Hebrew-speaking widows and the Greek-speaking widows. Here you have people who are Jewish Israelites and who don't speak the language.

Imagine. The children of Israel went to Egypt. They were there for four hundred years. That language was practically lost. Folks, in Babylon we know (according to Ezra) that when Ezra came back from Babylon to reestablish and to rebuild and to teach the people, this was just a seventy year period. Most of the people could no longer speak Hebrew. You and I both know that if you aren't constantly using your language, that you forget and have memory lapses.

Some people call these "Senior moments." It's like when you're trying to remember a word. I'm standing here sometimes and I have these and I'm not even a Senior yet. I'm trying to remember a word! It's because I've got so many words up there [Arthur points to his head], but if you're not using your vocabulary, you're losing your vocabulary.

For a person who knew a language and who emigrated – some people intentionally wanted to get rid of their accent so they couldn't be distinguished from where they came. Others just gradually lost it because they began to speak the language that they were immersed in more than the language from where they came.

You can see this in the first and second generations. It doesn't matter whether you're second generation Asian, second generation Hebrew, second generation Spanish or second generation whatever. You will find that individuals want to immerse themselves in the culture and blend in so they can become the culture and the environment that they live in. It's what happens.

So, the language was lost. Therefore, because the Greek language was being widely used, the translation of the Hebrew Scriptures was produced. Another reason was because many Jews spread throughout the empire were beginning to lose their language.

As translators performed their work on the Hebrew Bible, the Greek word most commonly used for "*bisar*" was "*euangelizesthai.*" In its most ancient usage, this Greek verb had many similarities with "*bisar,*" but it wasn't the same.

Like the Hebrew word, "*euangelizesthai*" was a word that was used to announce victory in battle; so it was a military term. You have to understand. This is where people sometimes use the phrases:

"Well, what that means...."

Or:

"That symbolizes..."

You know:

"This symbolizes that..."

Pretty soon once "this symbolizes that" enough, then **the symbol is being taught versus what it symbolizes**. Do you see how that works? This (which is actual) symbolizes this; and that (which is symbolizing) is separate from that which it symbolizes. Pretty soon the **symbol** is what is being taught and which becomes a **tradition**. Do you see?

"Well, the reason why we light the candles..."

"Well, the reason why we do the prayer like this..."

[Arthur waves his hands in the air toward his face as is done in Judaism to "usher in" the Sabbath.]

"Well, the reason why we put on the prayer shawl..."

"Well, the reason why we put the kippah on...the kippah symbolizes this. The prayer shawl symbolizes that. The candles symbolize that."

The symbols become the traditions and the traditions become what are taught!

Once the tradition is embedded in the culture, individuals have been moved from the *actual* and they are now practicing the *tradition*. This is why when Yeshua came on the scene he said:

"You people teach for commandments, the traditions of men and make the commandments of no effect!"

The people are practicing traditions and are thinking that they're keeping the commandments!

101

Because they're so connected and have identified with the tradition, *to attack the tradition is to attack the people that keep the tradition!* That's because they can't separate themselves from the traditions. Not only can the people not separate themselves from the tradition; the people who are taught that the Jews (get this) – when a person says that:

"The Old Testament is for the Jews…"

They have bought the tradition and drunk the Kool-Aid. Now they have been effectively separated from the foundation. If the foundation is destroyed, where would the righteous be? It is like building their houses upon sand. Those who are building their houses upon sand have the nerve to say:

"We who are living are the foundation of the Torah."

I don't know about you folks, but I'd rather have a solid foundation than sand. If I'm going to build, I'm going to build [on a solid foundation.] You see, sand just moves. You know what I'm saying. It's not solid.

Like the Hebrew word, *"euangelizesthai"* was a word that was used to announce victory in battle. The people made the connection that if we are in battle – you have to see how this works.

In times of old, there were two kinds of leaders. There were those who went into battle presumptuously because they believed they were "the people of God." Sometimes they got their butts whooped – badly!

Then there were the people who inquired of YeHoVaH whether they should go into battle. When the people were victorious in battle, they knew that their victory did not come from their own hands. Their victory came from YeHoVaH. **The battle is not ours. The battle is his!** You see.

"Not by might. Not by power but by my Spirit…"

Says YeHoVaH. These mentalities and mindsets associated "victorious in battle" to victory being ascribed or victory being given by YeHoVaH. So when a person experienced victory who believed in YeHoVaH, they knew that **their victory** (whatever it was) **came from whom? Him!**

Deliverance came from him. Salvation came from him. Victory came from him. Provision came from him. He fights our battles even today. Even today, believers ascribe victory in battle to YeHoVaH. It's a military term.

Another similarity could be found in that the Greek verb originally needed no direct object to convey the subject of the proclamation. The simple explanation is this.

"I bring to you, good news."

Now, if you came to me like that, do you know what my response is going to be?

"What is the good news?"

[Arthur laughs.] Do you hear what I'm saying?

"What IS the good news?"

So the words "good news" didn't necessarily need a subject. They stood by themself simply as "good news."

"Well, what is the good news?"

Now the "good news" needs a subject. That's when it evolved from the Hebrew and began to take its changes into the Greek. By the time the New Testament was written, the usage of *"euangelizesthai"* had changed slightly. It was just a little change.

I once heard somebody describe an airline flight or an airline pattern. I know that you all can't see this, but I'm going to do it anyway. [Arthur holds up a piece of paper and a pen to demonstrate a point.] If I'm in Charlotte [he points a pen to the lower left corner of the paper and makes a tiny dot] and I get on an airplane and I want to go to Los Angeles [goes to upper right and makes another dot], I need to go from here to here [points between the two dots].

I know that you can't see this. If that plane deviates slightly or just a little bit; five hundred or a thousand miles from now (just with a slight deviation) you will end up someplace other than where you are supposed to be. This stuff is important. Those of you who pay any attention to flights or even if you drive, you know this. Let's just use a simple idea like driving.

If I want to go from here to Chicago, I calculate the miles. I can see that my car gets a certain amount of miles per gallon, therefore I need a certain amount of gallons to get to Chicago.

I will need to stop at certain intervals to get gas. That's because where I am and where I need to be; my car doesn't carry that amount of gas. If I don't stop and get gas, what's going to happen to my car? It's going to stop somewhere on the side of the road!

Now, what if I'm in an airplane? It just falls out of the sky! If you sit on an airplane and you see these folks underneath [the plane on the outside tarmac], you'll notice that when the airplane comes in, some people come.

They have underground tanks. Ordinarily there's one guy who is going to bring this little tool. With it he is going to open up this thing in the ground and he's going to connect a hose. Then he's going to take that hose and connect it to the plane. Then he's going to start writing some numbers down to say:

> *"Okay, this plane is going to Los Angeles. It needs this amount of gas."*

> *"This plane is going to Chicago. It needs this amount of gas."*

When they fill out that bill, they are going to come onto the plane to give the pilot the bill. This is what is going to happen. You may not be paying attention to this, but it's just like going to the gas station. The pilot is going to get a bill for how much gas went into that plane. The pilot knows. This is why some people wonder:

"If the plane is going to a certain place and for whatever reason it turns around or it takes a detour and lands, why didn't it just go to its destination?"

Well chances are that it may not necessarily get there. Something has happened where the plane is malfunctioning, the plane has lost fuel or the plane won't get to its destination based on what [fuel] is in the plane.

"Why are you using planes?"

It is because when the word slightly deviated; imagine from the moment of that deviation to two thousand years later. It was supposed to end up over there. The gospel was on such a trajectory that by the time it got to [the year] 2017, we would be over there [Arthur points to his left].

But because of that "slight deviation," the people of YeHoVaH are totally off track. [Arthur points to his right.] They are in a place that they weren't designed to go. The sad thing about it is that many of them don't know. Why? That is because they are dependent upon people to tell them what to think and what to believe. Then they think that they came up with that belief on their own.

You see, here's how I know. I'm an intelligent person. Many of you in this room are intelligent people. But in our intelligence, we ended up in places that we realized were where we were not in the right place.

I think that one of the reasons why we get so upset is because **we realize that not only did people fool us, but we allowed ourselves to be fooled.** At some point you have to stop the foolery, which means that you have to take the responsibility of your faith walk into your own hands.

Now the gospel (which had no object) needs an object once it moves from the Hebrew to the Greek. This small shift in meaning explains why during the "Christian" era, a noun derived from the Greek verb became much more common. (It went from *"euangelizesthai"* to *"euanggelion."* This is from where we get the word "evangelist.")

Believers increasingly used *"euanggelion"* (the noun derived from *"euangelizesthai")* as a specific term to describe the good news of Yeshua.

"Euanggelion" was indeed the content of their preaching. However, because the Greek language now allowed the content of their proclamation to be separated from the idea of the "proclamation" itself, writers of the New Testament could also say that the good news was confessed. The good news was taught. The good news was spoken. The good news was told. The good news was announced and the good news was witnessed.

The word "gospel" ["*euaggelion*" {yoo-ang-ghel'-ee-on}] means: a reward for good tidings; good tidings. That word there seems to associate more with the word "*besowrah*" [(01309) {bes-o-raw'} or (shortened as) "*besorah*" {bes-o-raw'}] than with "*basar.*"

That's what it evolved into – a reward for good tidings. It wasn't just good tidings, but a *reward* for good tidings.

> *"Blessed are the feet of them who bring good news."*

It's not just the good news itself. It also means: the glad tidings of the Kingdom of Elohim soon to be set up and subsequently also of Yeshua the Messiah, the founder of this Kingdom. Now, notice this.

After the death of Christ [or Messiah], the term also comprises [and this is also in the definition] the preaching of (concerning) Jesus Christ as having suffered death on the cross to procure eternal salvation for the men in the Kingdom of God; but as restored to life and exalted to the right hand of Elohim in Heaven, thence to return in majesty to consummate the Kingdom of Elohim.

The usage of the word was as "gospel" forty-six times; as "Gospel of Christ" eleven times, "Gospel of God" seven times, "Gospel of the Kingdom" three times and with ten miscellaneous uses. When people go to their tools today, this is what they're going to see. They're going to see this usage. **This is a word usage that has been totally separated from its origin.**

Because there seem to be so many variables to the word "*gospel*," it becomes difficult to define. You can go out of here today and talk to people here and to folks who have listened to this message. You can ask five people:

"What is the gospel?"

See what they say. Chances are that you will get five different answers.

The gospel Yeshua preached is not the same as the gospel about Yeshua/Jesus. The definition of "gospel" has **evolved** from the original meaning to what it is today.

Development in English Translations

The earliest English editions of the Bible used the Anglo-Saxon word "*godspell*" to translate the noun "*euaggelion*." This was the original word in the Anglo-Saxon, which came from the Latin and the Greek to translate the noun "*euaggelion*." For those of you who remember reading in the gospel narrative when Yeshua was crucified, there was a placard over his head. How many languages were on that placard? Three. What were they? Latin, Greek and Hebrew.

What does that tell us? It says that in the day of Yeshua, people spoke three different languages. A person who spoke Latin (like the Romans who didn't speak Hebrew) would need a translator. The person who spoke Hebrew but who didn't speak Greek would need what? A translator. But nowhere in the Bible do you see translators translating (well, maybe in a couple of places). For the most part, the Bible is already translated for us.

This becomes a problem to a person who calls themself a student of Scripture. You are going to see that here in just a moment. This is a Bible. It's the *Tyndale New Testament* written in **1534**. In 1534, this is how it reads:

*Matthew 4:23 – "And **Iesus**..."*

Notice here that there is no letter "J," so how did "Iesus" become "Jesus?" This is 1534, ladies and gentlemen. In the 1611, it's the same thing.[6] *Iesous* came from the Greek. It is the Greek form of the KJV "Iesus" or "Jesus."

The **1534** *Tyndale New Testament* says:

> *"...went aboute all Galile teachyng in their synagoges and preachynge the **Gospell** of the kyngdome and healed all maner of sicknes and all maner dyseases amonge the people."*

That's the Old English. What's the word there? "Gospell." The letter "D" has dropped. This is the *PNT Bishop's New Testament* written in **1595**:

> *Matthew 4:23 – "And Iesus went about all Galilee, teaching in their synagogues, and preachying the **Gospell** of the kingdome, and healyng all maner of sicknesse, and all maner of disease among the people."*

Now, if you don't know this, you would assume that the King James (or whatever version of the Bible you have) is what everybody has always read from. In your mind you know that's not true, yet that doesn't stop you from thinking it. You have to connect to the people way back yonder. You both have to be on the same page to believe that what you believe today is what they believed way back then.

Some people don't even bother to make the connection **when the connection is detrimental to our faith.**

---

[6] In the 1611 King James Bible it reads "Iesus" at *Matthew 4:23.*

"Godspell" meant "the story about a god." It wasn't the story about *God*. It was the story about *a god*. **It was used because the story about Jesus was good news.**

What you're seeing here is that it is moving from what he preached to the story about him (and what he preached). That **slight deviation** right there is what has led us to where we are today.

This is one of the reasons why there is such a small group of individuals who are facing a large group of individuals who believe that the Gospel of "Jesus" is the gospel *about* Jesus. They say:

"Well, what's the difference?"

You are going to see that here in just a moment.

As English developed, the word was shortened to "gospel," and the Anglo-Saxon meaning was lost. If you thought for a moment that the "gospell" meant a story about a god, you would reject "godspell/gospell." As a matter of fact, you wouldn't even like the fact that "spell" is in the word! That's because it is associated with what? Witchcraft! Do you see? People who are big into symbols don't even make that connection.

Because *"euaggelion"* was used specifically to refer to the good news of Yeshua (or Jesus), some translators have used other words to translate *"bisar/basar"* in the Old Testament, even though the meaning of the two words are roughly the same.

This distinction has been drawn in order to differentiate between…

- the good news promised by the prophets

and

- the good news which Jesus actually brings.

Translators who make such a distinction often use "glad tidings" or an equivalent for the Hebrew.

The Change

In the New Testament, the word "gospel" has two variations of meaning:

1. The term is used to refer to the actual <u>message on the lips of Yeshua/Jesus</u> about the reign of Elohim/God (*Mark 1:14*), and

2. As the story told about Jesus <u>developed after</u> his death and resurrection.

The Good News/Gospel Evolved:

From – The words *Yeshua spoke* when he was alive and spoke;

To – The story told *about Yeshua* after his death, burial, resurrection and ascension.

This is what people will tell you that the "true" gospel is – the death, burial and resurrection of Jesus. They'll say:

> *"The gospel is about the death, burial and resurrection of Jesus."*

Now, I need you to understand something. **Yeshua spent a lot of time with his disciples, yet he didn't tell them about his death or his burial or his resurrection until the end of his ministry** (and they didn't believe him, even then). As a matter of fact, remember Peter? He rebuked it. He said:

> *"No! That ain't going to happen!"*

If the gospel is about the death, burial, and resurrection of Jesus, then **what was Yeshua preaching all of that time before he even mentioned that he was going to be persecuted? Was he <u>not</u> preaching the gospel?**

The average church person will tell you without a doubt that the gospel is about the death, burial, and resurrection of Jesus Christ. If you go to church and preach a sermon and you don't hear about the death, burial, and resurrection of Jesus Christ and then present an altar call for people to give their life to Jesus, then:

"You ain't preached the gospel!"

I grew up in that. That's what I grew up in. The death, burial, and resurrection of Jesus Christ become tantamount.[7] It becomes the focus of the gospel. The message goes like this:

"Hell-yes or Hell-no."

"Hell-yes if you don't give your life to Jesus. Hell-no if you give your life to Jesus."

What do you have? You have a fire and brimstone message.

"He died-uh! The devil thought he had 'em! Huh!"

[Laughter] That's what you hear. You know, you have some White preachers who try to get into that "Black preacher" thing. I mean, I used to stand in front of the mirrors and practice! Some of you all know what I'm talking about.

It was early Sunday morning. The preacher could preach and he could talk, but about fifteen minutes before the end of the message (or maybe ten minutes), folks are looking. It's like:

"Preacher, when are you going to preach?"

It's like:

"I've been preaching all along!"

"Well, you know, we need the CUE! Make the transition!"

Right?

Now it becomes *about* the death, the burial and:

"You need to give your heart to Jesus."

Then it leads to something like this:

"Every head bowed. Every eye closed. Nobody is looking around. You need to think about this

---

[7] This means "equivalent to."

for a moment because nobody knows what's going to happen to you when you leave here today. Today could be your last day on the planet and you have to make a decision today! Hell-yes or Hell-no."

I just came up with that yesterday, by the way. [Laughter] **But it'll preach!** [Arthur laughs.]

"How are you going to present this brother?"

"Hell-yes...or Hell-no! It's your decision!"

"If you leave here today without giving your life to Yeshua/Jesus, Oh Hell-yes will be your destination."

Nobody wants to go to Hell, right? I mean, think about it. You just heard a sermon for fifteen minutes about hell and what happens there and the demons and the fire that burns without quenching and the people who are thrown into the Lake of Fire and who spend an eternity in Hell.

You know that you don't spend an eternity in Hell because Hell and death are going to be cast into the Lake, but most of us heard those kinds of messages. Many of us who are older heard them. Many – I didn't say "all" of us who are older. We heard those kinds of messages.

If you go to a funeral and you hear them, they are saying:

"They gave their life to Jesus at an early age."

Now with young people today, you won't hear those kinds of funeral eulogies because they haven't given their life to Jesus. But for the most part, that's what you heard.

"They gave their life to Jesus at an early age."

I hear things today. You hear folks who have rejected God all of their lives, but now the eulogy is that they are "looking down from Heaven." You know?

"They are watching us right now. Their suffering is over. They're not suffering anymore."

I was watching a movie one day and I have to say that it was touching. I don't let them get into my spirit like that anymore, but I used to. It was a Public Broadcast Station show (PBS). They had this program on about a young boy who has Down's Syndrome. His mother died. They told the boy that his mother had "gone to be with God." That's what they told him. The boy wanted to know:

"Well, when is she coming back? When is she coming back from visiting God?"

You see, people don't understand, but we come up with various means trying to explain supernatural things to children. We are thinking that they don't understand. I'm going to tell you that children are a whole lot more sensitive than you think they are! They have a lot greater understanding than you think they do. They say things to you that boggle your mind. Don't under estimate a child!

Somebody said to me that **if a child is old enough to ask a question, then they're old enough to get an answer.** Do you hear what I'm saying? Don't lie to them! That's because once you tell them, they trust you to be telling them the truth.

You just planted a seed that they are going to grow up believing for the rest of their life. Then they find out that you lied. If they're old enough to ask a question, I just try them.

"Oh, you think that you're old enough to understand this answer?"

You just break it down [and they say]:

"Ah! Just...that's enough! I don't want to hear any more!"

"All right."

"You want to know where babies come from?"

[Laughter]

Halleluyah somebody, because if they don't know and you don't tell them the truth and you're talking about some birds and bees, they realize:

"Hey…"

Say what? [Arthur responds to an audience member's suggestion.] Oh, the stork! Yeah, the stork. Right, right. The stork.

So the story takes a change. It evolves. In other words, the message changed from:

What Yeshua *said*…to…a message *about* Yeshua.

The three gospels are:

1. The Gospel Yeshua preached/the Gospel of Yeshua

2. The Gospel about Yeshua

Then there's the:

3. Other gospel

You'll identify which one you got into.

The various versions of the Bible add to this confusion.

I just did a blanket count today. There is still some stuff that I've got laying around here, but right now I have access to sixty-five different versions of the Old and New Testaments. Which Bible version you use *matters.* This is why I will say to people that you can't trust your version. You really can't. People want to know the "best" and the "correct" version.

When I say that you can't trust your version, that doesn't mean to throw it away. It means that you have to understand that when you read what you read; you have to be able to study. If you're going to study and try to get to the root of what you're reading, you're going to need tools. You need the proper tools. You certainly don't try to cut a piece of wood with a steak knife. I mean, you'll be there all day. You'll probably be there all week, right?

You know those little knives with the serrated edge? You are out there just sawing away. If you have the right tool, you can rip right through that wood. But with the wrong tool, you'll just be sawing away. Right? So when it comes down to the right version or a study, you want to have the right tools to study, so your version matters.

I just want to take this one verse. It's *Hebrews 6:1*. I'll show you the difference. When a person hears "the gospel of," oftentimes what they hear is "the gospel about." **But there is a distinct difference between the gospel of and the gospel about.**

The gospel "of" is the gospel that Yeshua preached. The gospel "about" is the story about Yeshua's life. **These are two different things.**

Yeshua didn't come to tell us about his life! He came to preach the Kingdom of Heaven. And his gospel, his message starts with this word that people don't like hearing, which is:

"Repent."

No repentance? No salvation. You rarely hear that word in churches today. You rarely hear it in Messianic communities. You rarely hear it in Hebrew Roots communities. You rarely hear it any place where this book [Bible] is preached. Why?

Listen. Ministry needs money. Now, I hate to tell you this, but many of you have come to that conclusion. Some of us came to that conclusion the wrong way. Most people conclude that churches and preachers are all about money. I know that I did, so I can say this. To me, it was about "lucre." It was about money. It was about buying stuff. It was about:

"Bring your tithes. Bring your offerings."

And:

"Give us your money."

And that kind of thing. When it comes down to the gospel; in order for people to get money, what do they have to do? They have to preach the kinds of messages that make you feel good about giving.

You know, when you feel good, everybody's happy. Oh, you write a check. You put it in your pocket. If you think that you're going get something like a prophecy and somebody's prophesying or they have a line and you need to hear a word from God, then yeah, you're going to give!

But when it comes down to the kinds of messages that John preached and the kinds of messages that Yeshua preached and the kinds of messages that his disciples preached and the kinds of messages that Paul preached; those are the kinds of messages that will get you run out of town.

You read it! Read the gospels! You'll see. Read the gospel narratives! They weren't liked in a lot of places. There were people hunting for blood! There were people ready to take lives! You've got a mob of individuals that the Messiah came to save and who wanted him dead! For some reason or another, because of this watered-down gospel message about Jesus, all of that gets lost.

You don't hear the hypocrites, whitewashed sepulchers, dead men's bones, serpents or snakes. You don't hear those messages about people, you know? You certainly don't hear a message about repentance. **Preachers can't even tell the truth at a funeral.** They just put people into Heaven like they have that authority.

> *"Oh preacher, that was a good message! I know that 'Junebug' ain't in Heaven, but thank you for putting him there."*

[Laughter]

But Junebug didn't live like somebody who was Heaven-bound. Right? Everybody knows that Junebug isn't in Heaven. They know it!

> *"Hey, they say that Junebug's in Heaven. There's hope for me!"*

116

[Laughter] Right?

The Bible is *hard* on preachers. So if you are a ministry, the ministry needs money. You don't get people to give by preaching at them "hard."

Here's what I have found. **Yeshua had people that supported him.** He had resources and followers, even though the religious systems and institutions wanted him dead.

I wonder sometimes. Paul went all over the known world, collecting money. You know, he had money with him that he had collected from other places. He was taking it up to Jerusalem. I don't think that he had security.

He wasn't preaching some watered-down message! I'm thinking:

> *"You know, Paul, you're in a city. You've got the resources that you're taking to Jerusalem. Don't you think you need to take it easy in your message? Because if you keep preaching like that, you know that money that you are taking up to Jerusalem isn't going to make it."*

When they were lowering him down in the basket, they were lowering that money sack that he was carrying to Jerusalem right along with him. You see, there wasn't thinking like we have today where you have to have armour-bearers and fifteen people to guard you and all of that. **But that is what the gospel has become.**

> *Hebrews 6:1 – "Therefore leaving the principles..."*

This is the King James:

> *"...of the **doctrine of Messiah/Christ,** let us go on unto perfection; not laying again the foundation of repentance from dead works, and of faith toward Elohim,"*

Hebrews 6:1 in the New King James:

117

"Therefore, leaving the discussion of the elementary principles of Christ, let us go on to perfection, not laying again the foundation of repentance from dead works and of faith toward God,"

From **Webster's 1833 English Bible:**

*Hebrews 6:1 – "Therefore leaving the principles of **the doctrine of Christ/Messiah,** let us go on to perfection; not laying again the foundation of repentance from dead works, and of faith towards Elohim/God,"*

The **American Standard Version from 1901**:

*Hebrews 6:1 – "Wherefore leaving the **doctrine of the first principles of** Messiah/Christ, let us press on unto perfection; not laying again a foundation of repentance from dead works, and of faith toward God."*

This is where it gets a little tricky. The **New International Version:**

*Hebrews 6:1 – "Therefore let us move beyond the elementary **teachings about** Christ and be taken forward to maturity, not laying again the foundation of repentance from acts that lead to death, and of faith in God,"*

The **New Jerusalem Bible:**

*Hebrews 6:1 – "Let us leave behind us then all the **elementary teaching about** Christ and go on to its completion, without going over the fundamental doctrines again: the turning away from dead actions, faith in God,"*

The **Complete Jewish Bible:**

*Hebrews 6:1 – "Therefore, leaving behind the **initial lessons about the Messiah,** let us go on to maturity, not laying again the foundation of turning from works that lead to death,"*

118

Folks say:

"Why do you sell the Complete Jewish Bible?"

Because of its commentary value (and for the commentary). It's to help try to get people into a Jewish or a Hebrew-type of thinking to see how some of these individuals and traditions have actually been interpreted.

This is the *GWN* or *God's Word to the Nations:*

*Hebrews 6:1 – "With this in mind, we should stop going over the **elementary truths <u>about</u> Christ** and move on to topics for more mature people. We shouldn't repeat the basics about turning away from the useless things we did and the basics about faith in God."*

This is the *Tyndale New Testament* of 1534:

*Hebrews 6:1 – "Wherfore let vs leave the **doctryne pertayninge to the beginninge of a Christen man** and let vs go vnto perfeccion and now no more laye the foundacion of repentaunce from deed works and of fayth towarde God"*

This is the *New Living Translation* of 1862:

*Hebrews 6:1 – "So let us stop going over the **basic teachings <u>about</u> Christ** again and again. Let us go on instead and become mature in our understanding. Surely we don't need to start again with the fundamental importance of repenting from evil deeds and placing our faith in God."*

This is the *Basic English Bible* of 1949:

*Hebrews 6:1 – "For this reason let us go on from the **first things <u>about</u> Christ** to full growth; not building again that on which it is based, that is, the turning of the heart from dead works, and faith in God,"*

This is the *One New Man Bible* of 2011:

> *Hebrews 6:1 – "On this account, let us leave the* **elementary message** <u>**about**</u> **Messiah,** *for the maturity to which we should be brought, not again laying a foundation of repentance from dead works and faith in God"*

Do you see how it has moved to teachings *about* him? With respect to the "about" part, this is how it goes:

You teach a message about what he did. Now, what is the message? The message is *about* him. What he did and what he said did not deviate much, but what he said was more important than what he did. **What he did was to literally back up what he said.**

What Yeshua said is where we're going to find the *true* Gospel of the Kingdom; not in a message about him. That is because the message *about* him will tell you stories. **People come to church and they hear stories. That's what they get – stories!** And if you are animated in the telling of your story, or if you can tell a story in such a way that has your audience on the edge of their seat, it is like:

> *"Wow! I never heard that story told like that before!"*

What are we? We are children going into storytelling time! Next we're going to do "show and tell."

To know what the *true* gospel is, is to know and understand what Yeshua did and taught.

What did Yeshua preach? **Yeshua preached the Gospel of the Kingdom**. Others preach *about* Yeshua and at times they preach *about what Yeshua preached.*

Yeshua was the Messenger/Priest/King/Savior.

Yeshua was the message.

Yeshua preached the gospel.

Yeshua was the gospel.

The Message of the Gospel

The most basic summary of Yeshua's/Jesus' preaching appears in *Mark 1:15*. Here is what it says:

> *"The time is fulfilled,"*

He said:

> *"The kingdom of God is at hand: repent ye, and believe the gospel."*

Repent. These are words that Yeshua said. The Kingdom of Heaven, the Kingdom of Elohim is at hand. Whose Kingdom? Elohim's. **This is his Kingdom. This is his world.** What are we supposed to do?

The whole duty of man is to fear him and to keep his commandments. That's why we're here, ladies and gentlemen. Do you know what? If we are sincere about keeping his commands, if we are sincere in our walk with him, do you know that there is room for error?

Now, we don't want to live in error, but when we recognize error, we don't go and crucify ourselves. Just acknowledge it. It's painful to know that you did something wrong. But wisdom says:

> *"Hey. I did wrong. I repent. I learned from what I did and I'll move on and do my best not to repeat it."*

That's walking in faith! You see, the only way that you're not going to mess up is that you are perfect. How many perfect people are here? I see a foot. [Laughter] So we're working this thing out and we're walking this thing out. But in order for us to walk this thing out effectively, we have to have some kind of morals. We have to have some kind of guide. We have to have some kind of standards. The issue is this.

Who sets the standards?

In His Kingdom, He sets the standards. In our kingdom, we set them. In denominational kingdoms, they set them. This is where "statements of faith" come in. This is what "members in good standing" and contracts to become part of a ministry come in. That is because:

> *"A member in good standing abides by all of these rules and this is what we believe and this is what we say and this is what we teach. Everybody complies to that. Anybody who doesn't comply to this is a rebel."*

Do you see? What happens is that people have been taught to look for statements of faith.

> *"What do you all believe?"*

> *"What do you believe?"*

If you listen, what we believe will come out. If you find something contradictory to what is being said, then you can question it.

Let me ask you this question. Can anybody sum you up in twenty words or so? What about a couple of paragraphs? They can tell us everything about you. You can't tell us everything about yourself in a couple of paragraphs! Try to define yourself to somebody else so that when you are done, they know you perfectly.

The most basic summary of Yeshua's/Jesus' preaching appears in _Mark 1:15_. Now, get this. This is what _Mark_ says about Messiah:

> *Mark 1:15 – "The time is fulfilled."*

He said:

> *"The kingdom of Heaven/God is at hand: repent ye and believe the gospel."*

Get this. *Mark* offers no explanation of what the gospel is or what information it contains. Those of you who have your Bibles and your online Bibles and your cell phone Bibles, your iPad Bibles or your leather bound or paper bound Bibles or whatever Bibles you have; I just want you to see something really quickly.

This is *Mark* 1 verse 14. We just read it, but I want you to look at it because this next statement is important. It says:

> *Mark 1:14-15* – *"Now after that John was put in prison,"*

So John is put into prison. He's no longer out baptizing or preaching. Well, he is no longer out baptizing, but John is still preaching! [Arthur laughs]

> [14]*"...Yeshua came into Galilee, preaching the gospel of the kingdom of Elohim,* [15]*And saying, 'The time is fulfilled, and the kingdom of Elohim is at hand: repent ye, and believe the gospel.'"*

In my version it says: "the good news." Who has "good news" in their version? Raise your hand high so we can see it. [Counting audience members.] There are six. How many of you have "gospel" in your version? Okay, there's more than six. So we have "gospel" and we have "good news." Do you see this? The thing is that:

> *"Repent and believe the good news."*

[Turns into:]

> *"Believe the good news."*

> *"Believe the gospel."*

> *"Okay, I'll believe the gospel. Tell me, what is it?"*

If you notice, *Mark* doesn't offer [an explanation of] what the gospel is. There is no explanation of what the good news is or of which information it contains. You will see this throughout the gospel narratives.

> *"Believe the gospel."*

> *"Repent."*

> *"Believe the gospel."*

> *"Believe the gospel."*

"Well, what is the gospel?"

In the New Testament writings, you've got this idea of a gospel. Now you put in the blank, your version or definition of what you believe the gospel is because neither *Mark, Luke, John* nor *Matthew* explain. **But the preaching is:**

"Repent and believe."

"Repent and believe the gospel."

Well, what is the gospel, ladies and gentlemen? The closest that he comes to it is this:

"Repent."

Who is he speaking to? He's speaking to Hebrew people. He's speaking to the people of the book. **What do they have to repent from? It's because they have totally changed the nature and the structure of what YeHoVaH gave them to believe, into <u>something else</u>.**

They are being called, just like the prophets of old came. John the Baptist was a prophet forerunning Yeshua. Yeshua comes along and calls the people to repent, just like the prophets of old called the people to repent when they deviated or departed or walked away or went astray from YeHoVaH's commandments.

The readers who lived several centuries after the writing of the New Testament (us), must glean the message from careful study of all of its books.

In the next chapter we're going to look at the separation of the Testaments and its impact. When we get into the division of the Testaments, you have to understand. Some of us are still struggling and wrestling with some of this. The problem is that we've [typically] come out of the Sunday church where we weren't keeping any commandments.

We believed in the "Ten." Well, the ten minus one. We believed in the nine, but we didn't even really know how to keep those.

The churches that we were in had idols. They had things that we bowed down to. We were doing stuff and celebrating stuff that was idolatrous in nature.

We had no clue as to what we were doing, but we realized that the things that we were doing (about which we didn't have any clue) were wrong, so we made the transition. Some of us who have made the transition from that belief system into where we are today are still struggling with:

> *"How do I do this?"*

> *"What about all of these commands?"*

> *"You talk about all of these feasts. Why aren't we doing this? Why aren't we doing that? Why are we doing this and not that? Do we really have to do this? And if we're going to do it, how do we do it?"*

We're all trying to figure this stuff out. Are you hearing me? Oh, I know you are!

> *"Well, I'm just going to go along with the program, because I don't know what else to do."*

> *"I'm going to keep my mouth shut because I don't want to cause problems."*

> *"I'm not going to show my ignorance. You know, I just don't talk."*

These kinds of things are within us. Then when people outside of our environment start hitting us with some of this stuff, we don't know how to respond to it.

> *"Well, if you break one law, you break them all!"*

> *"If you don't do this right, you just messed the whole thing up!"*

> *"You can't keep the commandments, nobody can!"*

"You're trying to earn your salvation!"

"What about grace?" [8]

All of these things are going on within some of us. Some of us have resolved some of these issues. Some of us are still trying to figure some of this stuff out. Some of us don't know how to answer people, so we avoid them until we get some answers and then we can talk to them. Then they shoot stuff back at us that makes us go back and do some research (which is a good thing).

Let's be honest with ourselves. Forget everybody else. Let's at least start with being honest with ourselves so that what we do, we do with all of our heart. **You can't do what you do with all of your heart if your whole heart isn't in it**.

That's where I'm hoping that Dave, David, Efraiym and myself and others can help. We've got some tremendous teachings that have been made available to the brothers and sisters around the globe. I believe these resources will help aid people in their walk.

We don't have to be wandering around in the wilderness like we don't have any direction because we have so much to glean from. I think we're very fortunate. Halleluyah! We're establishing a place where people can become biblically literate in truth. That's what we're establishing. Amen.

In the next chapter we're going to talk about the separation of the Testaments. Where did this page come from [between the Old Testament and the New]? Do you see that page? This page is like a prison cell door. That's what it is. It separates the Old from the New.

This page has created mental blocks and spiritual blocks in the minds of people. Some people have come to conclude that the New Testament is the New Covenant. There are blocks that

---

[8] We offer a teaching called *What About Grace?* as a DVD and a print book in our online book store at www.ArthurBaileyMinistries.com.

we have that keep us from seeing the truth. We go into the book with blinders on. Then there are things that are established there to cause blinders to be secured.

We're going to see where that page came from and the separation. Then we're not going to physically rip it out, but we're going to subliminally, mentally, emotionally and psychologically rip that thing out of our minds so that we can see one seamless set of writings and make the connection.

That's because one without the other is incomplete; no matter how you look at it. The separation of the Testaments and its impact is what we'll explore in the next chapter.

✫ **Part Four** ✫

The Separation of the
Testaments and its Impact

Here is what won't be in this book or on the video or on the *PowerPoint* slides. It is what Father will speak to you through the course of the broadcast or the reading of this book. If you don't capture it, there is a good chance that you'll lose it. The word of YeHoVaH is too precious to lose, so you want to have something to write on and to write with, in case he speaks.

One way that you can practically guarantee that he will speak is that before you begin, to [always] ask him.

> *"Speak to me."*

Halleluyah. I'm going to tell you that he wants to speak to you more than you want to be spoken to. If you give him the permission to speak to you, there is a very, very good chance that he will speak to you and give you a message. He will give you a word before you are done. What I say will be on the video [or in the book]. What you will need to capture is that *Rhema,* that word that Father speaks to you and to your mind, to your head and to your spirit. That again, is what you want to capture.

Here we're going to highlight a little bit of the cultures, customs and languages and show you how these things divide. Recently I was sharing with one of my brothers that one of the challenges of this particular series that I am teaching is that it is more or less an academic teaching. It is more or less something that you would expect if you were in a Seminary class or a Bible College class. The challenge is that this [day] is a Sabbath.

Most of us (especially those of us who grew up in church or around church) have been accustomed to coming to church to hear a sermon. In some environments that I have been in, if the sermon is not presented in a certain way (with a little whooping), the sermon "isn't" really a sermon. It's a talk. Some of you all know what I'm talking about.

I've got this challenge of taking a message that would be designed for academia, to bring it on a Sabbath morning and put it into a sermon context while teaching and hoping that you retain the teaching. The things that we're revealing to you (and have revealed to you over the last three chapters) – I'm telling you. This is some phenomenal stuff. I see that as I go back and listen to it. That's not because I'm preaching and teaching it. It is because of what the Almighty is leading me to and giving me to share with you, his people. Amein?

Here we're going to talk a little bit about cultures, languages and customs. Then we're going to get into the separation of the Testaments. We are going to look at the impact that it has had on Americans who have pretty much translated the gospel or the Bible of the American version of the Bible into every language, and exported it into practically every nation.

What goes with the translation is the American culture. This is why if you travel anywhere in the world today – it doesn't matter where you go in the world. If there is a so-called "church," if there is a so-called "preacher," if there is a so-called "congregation," nine times out of ten, that congregation is going to be fashioned after what you see, here in America.

Why? It is partly because the culture of the American Gospel has also been inundated in the translations of the American Gospel and exported around the world. Let's look at it.

When YeHoVaH confused the languages (back in *Genesis*), he made it difficult for men to communicate. Amongst people who speak the same language is the immerging [disappearance] of customs, culture and traditions. Today these customs, cultures, languages and traditions manifest among people of different races and geographies, both nationally and internationally.

As missionaries, David and I and Simona at times have travelled. We encounter various customs, cultures and traditions among the various groups of people that we minister to. These customs, cultures and traditions that are developed among people of different languages create this sense of pride. There are rivalries and ultimately, wars such as world wars, civil wars and I could even go on to say turf wars.

Whenever you live in a metropolitan area or an area where you have large groupings of various people; you will find that not only do people have a tendency to separate themselves among races and languages, but they also have a tendency to separate themselves among their cultures.

Even among races that separate are people within those races who are a certain age and that have a particular culture. It may be the art culture, the music culture or the night life culture. You will find that these cultures have a tendency to pop up.

In certain communities you have groupings of individuals who develop what are called gangs. Within these gangs there are gang symbols and gang language. You'll see the graffiti and how they mark up certain neighborhoods to let you know of their presence. These things create fear, but they also cause pride among the people. What this pride does is that it has a way of saying:

"We are better than you."

It creates these superiority and inferiority complexes.

As the followers of Yeshua came together in the first century, there were basically two groups of followers within the fellowship. There were:

1. The *Grecians*

These were Hellenists; those born in lands other than Palestine (or what we know of today as Israel) who spoke the Greek language and who were more Grecian than Hebraic in their attitudes and outlooks.

How many of you have ever seen a movie that came out several years ago called *My Big Fat Greek Wedding*? If you saw that movie, raise your hand. The majority of you in this room saw that movie. In all of my travels and with all of my communications with people, I have found two groups of people among the world's people that probably have the greatest

131

amount of pride than any other group of people that I have ever met.

One group are the Jews – Jews who identify and who claim as being the "chosen." These are those who were designated by the Almighty to be a light to the world and to teach and rule the world. They see themselves as ones who have influenced all of the world religions, especially the main religions: Judaism, Christianity and Islam. That is one of the greatest groups of prideful people that I have ever met.

The second group who are probably even more prideful than the Jews are the Greeks. That's because the Greeks feel that they have influenced every culture on the planet and every language that is known to man.

What is interesting is that you have these two groups in one community called the "New Testament church" or the "first century community" of believers. Within that group we see that these issues rise up.

The second group were:

2. The *Hebrews*

These are Hebraic individuals, those who spoke the Aramaic and/or Hebrew languages of Palestine and who preserved the Jewish culture and customs.

Now, in one first century congregation, there were the Greeks who felt that they had influenced all of the cultures; and the Hebrews, the Jews, who felt that they had influenced all of the world's religions.

> *Acts 6:1 – "And in those days, when the number of the disciples was multiplied, there arose a murmuring of the **Grecians** against the **Hebrews**, because their widows were neglected in the daily ministration."*

It didn't take long after the Messiah to get to the point where these cultural clashes, tribal clashes and these individuals who were of two separate groups began to discriminate against one another. The interesting thing is that the dominancy was among the Hebrews. Why? It was because the apostles were Hebrew and they all grew up in the land of Israel.

Now there are those who, after the community begins to grow, come together. Most of these Greek-speaking Hebrews begin to clash with the Hebrew-speaking Hebrews. Why is there an issue? It's because there's a language barrier. There is a cultural barrier and there are customs.

They begin to complain. They didn't just complain. They didn't complain. They murmured. There's a difference between complaining and murmuring. When there is a complaint, individuals usually lodge their complaint. But murmuring is complaining among one another; not the individuals who have the ability or the authority to invoke change.

It came that there was murmuring of the Grecians against the Hebrews because:

> *Acts 6:1 – "And in those days, when the number of the disciples was multiplied, there arose a murmuring of the **Grecians** against the **Hebrews**, because their widows were neglected in the daily ministration."*

The word there "*Hellenistes*" [hel-lay-nis-tace'] 1) Hellenist is 1a) one who imitates the manners and customs or the worship of the Greeks, and uses the Greek tongue; 1b) used in the New Testament of Jews born in foreign lands and speaking Greek. They are referred to three times as "Grecians" in the New Testament.

The word for Hebrews or "*Hebraios*" [heb-rah'-yos] means: 1) Hebrew; 1a) any one of the Jewish or Israelitish nations; 2) in a narrower sense, those who live in Palestine and who use the language of the country; 3) all Jewish Christians, whether they spoke Aramaic or Greek. The word is used as "Hebrews" five times.

Let me expound upon this whole idea of "Israelitish" just for a moment. You see, a Jew was part of the Hebrew people. All

Hebrews were not Jews and all Jews were not Hebrews. Why? There is a word in the New Testament called a "proselyte." A proselyte is a person who has converted to Judaism. They were a non-Hebrew, a Gentile who converted to Judaism; which made them Jewish but they weren't from the tribe of Judah nor were they of the Hebrew people. They simply converted.

Just because a person calls themself a "Jew" doesn't mean that they are of the tribe of Israel. This is important. This is why several years ago I would say to you all that if somebody introduced themself – this is the other thing. You're not in a conversation with a Greek person very long before you know that they're Greek. You're certainly not in conversation with a Jewish person very long before they let you know that they're Jewish.

When a person introduces themselves to me and they say:

"Well, I'm Jewish..."

And I didn't ask them, then I ask them:

"What tribe are you from?"

"What do you mean? I'm Jewish!"

We're already established that. What tribe?

Acts 6:2-5 – "Then the twelve called the multitude of the disciples unto them, and said, 'It is not reason that we should leave the word of Elohim, and serve tables.' ³Wherefore, brethren, look ye out among you seven men of honest report, full of the Holy Ghost and wisdom, whom we may appoint over this business. ⁴But we will give ourselves continually to prayer, and to the ministry of the word. ⁵And the saying pleased the whole multitude: and they chose Stephen, a man full of faith and of the Holy Ghost, and Philip, and Prochorus, and Nicanor, and Timon, and Parmenas, and Nicolas a <u>proselyte</u> of Antioch:"

Nicolas has gone through two conversions. First, he has gone from the Gentile to the Judaism conversion. Now he's come to believe that Yeshua is the prophesied Messiah first established in the Torah, then promulgated through the teachings of the prophets.

> Acts 6:6-7 – *"Whom they set before the apostles: and when they had prayed, they laid their hands on them. [7]And the word of Elohim increased; and the number of the disciples multiplied in Jerusalem greatly; and a great company of the priests were obedient to the faith."*

So there was a great company of priests (these are Levites) who became obedient to the faith.

During the time of Yeshua's ministry, before his death, burial, and resurrection and after his resurrection, there was only one Testament. **During the time of the apostles' ministry, the Book of *Acts*, the early church (the first congregation of believers) and the first two hundred years of ministry, there was only one Bible Testament: the Old Testament.**

You may say:

> *"Why are you emphasizing that?"*

Just stick with me. **The New Testament did not exist during the time of the apostles' ministry, so they didn't preach from the New Testament!**

Why?

Because it didn't exist!

Peter preached from the Old Testament. The Apostle Paul preached from the Old Testament. They were teaching what the Torah and the prophets taught, concerning Yeshua. Peter's first sermon was from the *Psalms* in the Old Testament. Here it is in *Acts 1:15*. He says:

> Acts 1:15 – *"And in those days Peter stood up in the midst of the disciples,"*

135

This is after Messiah had been crucified, resurrected, ascended, and [before he left he] had told them to wait for the Holy Spirit (the promise that the Father had promised).

> *"...and said, (the number of names together were about an hundred and twenty,)* [16] *'Men and brethren, this scripture'"*

What Scripture?

> *"'...must needs have been fulfilled,'"*

Now he lets us know that he is going to be speaking about a Scripture.

> *"'...which the Holy Ghost by the mouth of David'"*

Now we know that it was David writing.

> *"'...by the mouth of David spake before concerning Judas,'"*

They interpret that David warned them of Judas. This is what Peter is saying.

> *"...which was guide to them that took Yeshua."*

> *Acts 1:17 – "For he was numbered with us, and had obtained part of this ministry."*

> *Acts 1:18 – "Now this man purchased a field with the reward of iniquity;"*

That was the thirty pieces of silver for which he had betrayed Messiah.

> *"...and falling headlong,"*

Now, he didn't actually purchase it. Somebody else purchased it using the money that he ultimately rejected.

> *"...and falling headlong, he burst asunder"*

In other words, he committed suicide. It is as if he jumped to his death. Now, I know that in the movie *The Passion of the Christ,* they have him hanging from a rope. But it says that he:

"...falling headlong,"

That means **head first.**

"...he burst asunder in the midst, and all his bowels gushed out."

Acts 1:19 – "And it was known unto all the dwellers at Jerusalem; insomuch as that field is called in their proper tongue, Aceldama, that is to say, 'The field of blood.'"

Acts 1:20 – "For it is written in the Book of Psalms, Let his habitation"

There it is.

"...written in the Book of Psalms, Let his habitation be desolate, and let no man dwell therein: and his bishopric let another take."

Peter was quoting from *Psalms.*

Psalms 69:25 – "Let their habitation be desolate; and let none dwell in their tents."

Psalms 109:8 – "Let his days be few; and let another take his office."

Or his bishopric or his position.

Peter's second sermon was from the prophet Joel and the Psalmist/Prophet David. That was David who wrote the *Psalms* and who was a king.

Acts 2:14-16 – "But Peter, standing up with the eleven, lifted up his voice, and said unto them, 'Ye men of Judaea,'"

This is after the Holy Spirit had been given. Individuals were speaking in "unknown" languages. People were hearing them in their own tongues and individuals accused them of being under the influence of alcohol. Why? Because it was a festival where they were permitted to eat and drink in the presence of the

Almighty, so they were being accused of either drinking all night, or drinking early in the morning. It says:

> "'...and all ye that dwell at Jerusalem, be this known unto you, and hearken to my words: [15]For these are not drunken, as ye suppose, seeing it is but the third hour of the day.'"

It's too early.

> [16]"'But this is that which was spoken by the prophet Joel.'"

Now Peter stands up in the midst of all of the people and declares what was spoken by the prophet Joel and he is actually declaring it from memory. You have to understand something, ladies and gentlemen. These were ignorant and unlearned men, yet he has memorized Scriptures.

How did he learn it? He learned it from his Messiah, the Master. Why? Because the entire time that Yeshua was with them, what was he teaching from? He was teaching from the Torah, from the *Psalms* and from the prophets. I will show you here.

> *Acts 2:25 – "For David speaketh concerning him, 'I foresaw the Lord always before my face, for he is on my right hand, that I should not be moved...'"*

Here he says "from David":

> *Acts 2:30-31 – "Therefore being a prophet, and knowing that Elohim had sworn with an oath to him, that of the fruit of his loins, according to the flesh, he would raise up Messiah to sit on his throne; [31]He seeing this before spake of the resurrection of Messiah, that his soul was not left in hell, neither his flesh did see corruption."*

After the resurrection, the apostles continue to go to the temple for prayer. If you remember what Peter prayed or what Peter said in *Joel*, he said:

"These men are not drunk, but this is that which the prophet Joel prophesied; that in the last days YeHoVaH was going to pour out his Spirit on all flesh."

All flesh. Sons and daughters were going to prophesy. Young men would see visions. Old men would dream dreams. And:

"Upon my servants and my handmaidens will I pour out my Spirit and they will…"

Do what? They will prophesy. So prophesying, prophesy, hearing from YeHoVaH and speaking for YeHoVaH is a sign of YeHoVaH's Spirit dwelling in us. That is every last one of us. This is why Paul wrote. He says:

"You may all prophesy!"

Why? Because you've all been given the ability to hear for yourself, the mouth of YeHoVaH. Now, I'm going to show you something here in just a moment that is going to solidify this fact, but you have to embrace this fact. You really have to. The reason why you have to embrace this fact is because every last one of us in this room; if we commit ourselves to it, we have the ability to get in the presence of the Almighty and talk to him and he will talk to us!

This was part of his plan! From the very beginning in the garden, what did he do? He communed with his creation. Mr. and Mrs. Adam talked to him. He talked to them. Their children heard from the Almighty. Remember the conversation with Cain?

"Cain? What's wrong with you, man? Why is your face fallen? If you do well, will you not be accepted?"

But he says:

"Sin crouches at your door, but you must…"

What?

"…MASTER it."

139

YeHoVaH gave Cain the ability to master sin. This is what he did. If you don't master it, what is going to happen? It is going to master you. This is what happens. If you don't control sin, sin will control you.

Do you know who sins? Sinners. This is why I reject the notion:

"I'm a sinner saved by grace."

That's because if I'm a sinner saved by grace, what am I dependent upon? I'm dependent upon grace. Why? Because I'm going to sin. **I'm the righteousness of YeHoVaH. You are the righteousness of YeHoVaH.** We are to seek first, what? His Kingdom and his righteousness.

How you see yourself is vital to your walk. Some of you all see yourselves as "no good." That's not you all [in the audience or reading this book]. You all have heard enough teaching. I'm just talking to people who have just joined us today [to hear the broadcast or who are reading this book]. Right?

You have heard so much teaching that it is to the point where you know that you've been invited to be perfect. You've been invited to be holy. You've accepted the invitation to be holy. You've accepted the invitation to be perfect or to work on being perfected. You've also come to the conclusion that you know that he is righteous and he has called you to be righteous.

We're to seek his righteousness and his Kingdom. Then all of the stuff in the world that the Gentiles spend all of their time running after will be added to us. Let's not put the cart before the horse. Stop running after stuff. Run after *him*. If we run after him, he'll give us the stuff, but you can't handle the stuff if you don't have him first.

Why? Because the stuff will have you. You can't even leave home without worrying about your stuff. Stuff is stuff! You can't take it with you. You can't take it with you on vacation. You certainly can't take it with you when you leave here. All of the stuff that you've been worried about for all of this time, when you die, somebody else is going to take your stuff. They're not going to care about your stuff the way that you care about it.

Think about some folks. They spend all of this money on some art. Their children inherit it but they don't have a clue as to what it is. That art that you didn't want anybody to touch is in a box at Goodwill. You've got folks rolling over in the [grave]. They ain't rolling over in their graves because they don't even know that their stuff is the in the box. They're dead! They aren't looking down. They aren't even looking up! [Laughter] Halleluyah, y'all! Are we there yet? We're getting there.

Acts 3:1. Now get this, folks. In *Acts 3:1* we anticipate that maybe fifteen years have passed. We don't really know the timeline, but we know that many years have passed between *Acts 2* and *Acts 3.* Peter and John went up together. Where did they go?

> *Acts 3:1 – "Now Peter and John went up together into the temple at the hour of prayer, being the ninth hour."*

Into the temple. When? At the hour of prayer. We know what hour that was. That was the ninth hour. Why are they going up to the temple? They're going up to the temple to pray. Right? Why? The Jewish temple? Get this.

> **Please note: The disciples, the apostles continued to go to the temple even after the veil of the temple separating the Holy place from the Holy of Holies had been ripped.**

Now, I know that some of you all have seen the movies that show that during the time that Yeshua was crucified, the temple was shaken and bricks and everything [were falling] and the whole temple was discombobulated [upset]. Everything was just broken or cracked. That's what the movies show us. Unfortunately, that's where many people get their theology: from the movies.

Here's what happened. This was when Yeshua was crucified:

Matthew 27:51 – "And, behold, the <u>veil of the temple was rent in twain</u>"

In other words, it was rent in two. Notice this.

"...from the top to the bottom; and the earth did quake, and the <u>rocks rent</u>;"

One would have to ask:

"What do the rocks renting have to do with the earth quaking?"

But you see, here's the thing that we pointed out to you all. Remember Solomon's Temple? In the wilderness, the Almighty called Moses. Moses was to get individuals who were to fashion the furniture that went into the temple. The Holy of Holies had the Ark of the Covenant. When Solomon's Temple was destroyed, the Ark of the Covenant disappeared.

From the [time of] Temple of Solomon [forward], there was no more Ark in the temple. Now, two temples existed after that. Israel went into Babylonian captivity. They were released. They came back into Israel and built Zerubbabel's Temple and reinstituted the Levitical priesthood.

The high priest would go into the Holy of Holies, and this was for years. It is anticipated that almost four hundred years [passed]. For over four hundred years (from the time of Zerubbabel's Temple to Herod's Temple), year after year (over four hundred-plus times), the high priest went into the Holy of Holies and performed the high priest's duties once a year, on Yom Kippur. There was no Ark, so what was he doing? He was going through the motions.

But when Zerubbabel's Temple was built, guess what they put in place of the Ark? Rocks! Rocks. Which may be these very rocks that were rent when the Temple veil was rent. One would have to ask:

"What's the high priest doing back there?"

The thing about it is that the only person during the lifetime of that high priest who even knew what was back there (other

142

than the ones who rebuilt the temple structure and who placed the curtains up and put whatever was back there, back there) were the few high priests. They were the only ones who knew. So if there were hundreds of thousands of priests (Levites) working in the temple, none of them ever saw what was behind that curtain until it was rent.

Now, when it was rent, what could have happened? The high priest no longer had a job (per sea, unless they put it all back together and keep the façade going), but everybody (all the Levites, all the priests) at that moment could see what was back there. There was nothing there but rocks. How do we know this?

According to the Mishnah (*Middot* iii. 6), the "Foundation Stone" stood where the Ark used to be, and the high priest put his censer on it on Yom Kippur. The **Foundation Stone** ("Rock") is the name of the rock at the center of the Dome of the Rock in Jerusalem.

For any of you who go to Israel, if you go up onto the Temple Mount, there is this place where you used to go in, but you're not allowed to go in anymore. Inside is where you find the Dome of the Rock. This is supposed to be the place where Abraham ascended to take and sacrifice Isaac. It was (so they say) also the actual place where the Holy of Holies was supposed to have existed; although a few meters away from there is another place that they say could have been it.

That Dome of the Rock is supposed to have been the rock that was supposedly in the Holy of Holies after Zerubbabel's Temple was built. The Bible says that the veil was rent and the rock was rent.

Where Has the Power Gone?

As the message of the gospel has evolved from its original presenter, the power that accompanied the message has been diminished. The signs and wonders that used to follow the believers no longer follow them. The presenters of the gospel have become more intellectual and powerless, just as the gospel has become more about knowledge without power.

The Apostle Paul seemed to have issued a subtle warning when he stated that:

> *"My preaching was not with enticing words of man's wisdom, but in demonstration of the Spirit and of power:"*

What does that mean? Paul said:

> *"Listen. You know, the words? They're fine, but let me show you the gospel. Let me show you the power that accompanies the gospel."*

Yeshua walked in that authority and power. The disciples walked in that authority and power. Paul walked in that authority and power. We find that the early congregation, all of the way up until *Acts 8* walked in that authority and power. It seems like once the Bible (as they say) "was completed" – by the way, it's not completed, because the *Acts* of the Apostles are still acting out!

Here is what Peter (who stood up) said about this power that was poured out on Pentecost:

> *"The promise is for you, for your children and for your childrens' children...as many as YeHoVaH our Elohim will call."*

So to this day, the outpouring, the baptism of the Holy Spirit, the power of the Holy Spirit, the signs and wonders that are supposed to follow believers; unless you're not a believer, then it's okay for signs and wonders not to follow you.

> *"But these signs shall follow them that believe."*

If you are a believer, you are supposed to be demonstrating power unless you have been taught that intellectual gospel that has no power. This is why people argue about doctrines. They are fighting all day long about doctrines.

> *"Well, you know, brother, that ain't what [the Bible says]..."*

What you need to have is the authority and the power to demonstrate the authority. You see, when you demonstrate power, you get people's attention a lot more quickly than with your intellect.

I told you that when David and I and Simona were sent to Israel to be missionaries and to travel through the land and to teach and preach, Father specifically said:

> *"Don't teach doctrine. Demonstrate my power.*
> *Demonstrate my power."*

You see, when your prayers get results, guess who people look for when they need to get a prayer through? But there are too many people who are looking for people to get a prayer through because their prayers don't get through. Why is that? A lot of it is because of what we've been taught, folks. I stand and try to teach people about the power. It has to penetrate all of those cores and layers of unbelief.

That's because many of you came from churches and from denominations that I came up through. There was no power there. None! In the Pentecostal churches, it seemed like the power that they had was to give you a word of prophecy for a certain amount of money, and elaborate tongues. You could talk in tongues all day long.

> *"Hah hah hah hah..."*

Don't make me go there. Man, I'll tell you. It used to sadden me as I was part of this (I thought at the time) very powerful church. People were trying to impress one another and I got caught up in it. You know if you are praying publicly in a congregation, you are leading intercessions. You see, that was the difference.

> *"We're doing intercession. This is intercessory*
> *worship."*

You know, it's that time of worship, about thirty minutes before the service. All of the leaders get together and gather. They want to "set the environment" for the worship service.

They invite the intercessors and the intercessors are walking around.

> *"Oh, robo-schtack-uh-hah! Lah-buh-ras-kah! Ash-tu-did-ee-gosh-tah!"*

[Fake tongues]

You all know what I'm talking about! [Laughter] You know, I'm not trying to be funny. I'm just trying to take you back.

And in all of this power, there is all of this witchcraft, fornication, lying and backbiting, meanness and spite. This is in the midst of all of that "Holy Ghost power." You see, when the Spirit of YeHoVaH shows up, *that foolishness can't stand* in the midst of that. There is no evidence in the Bible where foolishness was able to stand in the presence of the Almighty when he showed up. As a matter of fact, when he showed up, folks usually fell on their face.

I will tell you that I was in churches for years and I never saw anybody fall on their face until they had *fallen.* Now all of a sudden they want to cry out at the altar (and that's good). That's good when you fall and cry out at the altar, but when you get up, there should be some kind of change. You don't want to spend your life at the altar.

There are folks who are "saved by grace." **No, we're supposed to walk in power!** Grace is for when you fall. That's what grace is for, ladies and gentlemen. Grace is Father's mercy and favor. This is why the gospel is so important. It is because the Good News, the gospel that we're talking about, is a gospel first of all that leads off with "Repent!" A gospel without repentance "ain't no gospel." It's not the *true* gospel. It may be a gospel, but it's that *other* gospel.

When we repent, what happens? The Father's power comes. Now we have to walk in it. So it says:

> *1 Corinthians 2:4 – "And my speech and my preaching was not with enticing words of man's*

wisdom, but in demonstration of the Spirit and of power:"

Why?

1 Corinthians 2:5 – "That your faith should not stand in the wisdom of men, but in the power of YeHoVaH."

This is where people are in denominationalism. **Their faith is standing in the wisdom of men.** This is why when men in denominations fall, people fall. It's because their faith is in the person. I've seen it. Pastors fall and their churches implode. The next thing you know, it doesn't exist anymore.

People's lives are a mess. Why? It's because they were looking to their leader, who should have been pointing them to the Master. Our eyes are supposed to be on the one who is the author and finisher of our faith! I've been in places where individuals have fallen and I have seen individuals fall because their leaders fall and it's like:

"What's wrong with you all?"

That's letting me know, and it should let you know who their faith was in. That's because those who add to their faith; that which Peter talks about, he says:

"They shall never fall."

You've got the ability to deny the devil! Why? Because you've been given authority over the devil. The devil is supposed to be under *your* feet! That's not pride and arrogance. It should make you humble! That's because it's not coming from you. It's coming from him. **The authority and power you walk in comes from him, not from you, not from me and not from any preacher.**

Your relationship should be more focused on him than on each other. When your relationship with him is intact, then you'll know how to honor and respect one another. You'll quit the gossiping. You'll quit the murmuring. You'll quit the complaining. You'll quit the backbiting. You'll quit all of that mess. That is not supposed to be a part of the body of Messiah to begin with! Halleluyah! Don't make me fuss.

There's just too much mess going on among saints.

> *1 Corinthians 2:6 – "Howbeit we speak wisdom among them that are perfect: yet not the wisdom of this world, nor of the princes of this world, that come to nought:"*

> *1 Corinthians 2:7 – "But we speak the wisdom of Elohim in a mystery, even the hidden wisdom, which Elohim ordained before the world unto our glory:"*

We receive his glory and then we glorify him. How? With your lifestyle.

The dry, dead, intellectual message of the American Gospel has produced dry, dead, intellectual messages.

I know that I'll get some flack on this, but that's all right. Before there was a New Testament, there was the Old Testament known as the Tanakh.

According to the Talmud – I know that I've quoted the Mishnah and the Talmud and I don't generally do that, but again, here we are in an academic environment, preaching. But according to the Talmud, much of the Tanakh was compiled by the men of the Great Assembly. It was a task that was completed in 450 BCE.

"BCE" is "before the common era," or actually before Messiah. Folks said that B.C. was talking about "before Christ," but that came later. After that, folks didn't want to be identified with Christ, so they came up with "before the common era." Then C.E. or common era, which is A.D., or "after the death." It has remained unchanged ever since.

The Tanakh consists of twenty-four books. You may say:

> *"Well, wait a minute."*

Before you go there, let me tell you. It counts as one book each: *1* and *2 Samuel* are counted as one book. It counts *1* and *2 Kings* as one book. It counts *1* and *2 Chronicles* as one book and it counts *Ezra* and *Nehemiah* as one book. It also counts the twelve Minor Prophets as a single book. That's the way the Tanakh counts it.

Rabbinic Judaism recognizes the twenty-four books of the Masoretic Text (commonly called the Old Testament, the Tanakh or the Hebrew Bible), as authoritative. Modern scholarship suggests that the most recently to be written are the books of *Jonah, Lamentations* and *Daniel,* all of which may have been composed as late as the second century BCE.

I'm going to step out here onto a limb for a moment, because it's so important. The reason why I want to help believers get solid in their faith, in their walk and in their knowledge and understanding of Scripture is so that you don't have to be afraid to question Scripture. You see, if you're like me, you've heard that this book is the "infallible word of Elohim." If that's what you've been taught, then you have probably come to the conclusion that everything in this book came straight out of the mouth of Elohim.

We know better than that! You see, questioning the Bible is not questioning the Almighty. Understand something folks. Please see this image.

YeHoVaH did not write this Bible and hand it down to Earth to somebody who found it!

They weren't hiking one day and came across silver or golden tablets and who said:

"Voila! We have found the word of 'Gawd!'"
[God]

It didn't happen like that, but there are people who want you to think that way because they don't want you to think. As long as you don't think, they've got you. If you don't think, you take what they say as if it's the gospel truth and:

"You don't question the authority of Gawd!"

"Are you questioning my authority?"

"No, I'm questioning what you teach because my Bible doesn't say what you just said!"

"Oh, I've been at this for the last twenty years. Have you gone to Seminary?"

"What's that got to do with anything?"

I mean, what does the degree you have, have to do with anything? I know people who have degrees and who disagree with you. Any of you who have PhDs, Doctorates and Masters; you could work alongside other people in the same field with the same degree that you have, and disagree. It happens folks. Why?

That's because how you've seen things and how you've heard things are different than how somebody else heard it. We hear and see based on how we have been brought up. If you've been brought up in a prejudiced environment, then you [may] see everything through a prejudiced lens.

This is why I don't fault my Caucasian brothers who don't understand what it means to grow up in the Black community. That's because they can't see things the way I see things. They see things through their eyes and will never be able to see things through my eyes. Nor will I ever be able to see things through their eyes.

Your community, your environment, your upbringing is what [often] affects how you see and how you interpret what you see. This is one of the reasons why – this is only done in the military, as far as I know. People go to universities and into higher education and bring their little [bit of] knowledge with them. Professors have a way of breaking down their knowledge and showing them the "fallacy" of their information. They fill their heads with new information, but it doesn't break down the Spirit.

A person who has a faith can go into a theological environment and hold onto their faith because they believe their faith is solid. They will not let anybody take that faith away from them, even though they're in an institution that may be preaching a different denominational aspect than what they went in with. If our children are solid when we send them into the institutions, they won't allow the institutions to dismantle them.

But in the military, everybody gets broken down.

"Maggots!"

I mean, you know. We all become "maggots" in boot camp! [Arthur laughs.] Do you know what I'm saying? It's like:

> *"You don't have an opinion. If I want to know what you think, I'll tell you."*

The whole point I'm trying to make is that when it comes down to questioning things, we all should be questioning things that we see don't align. Get this. *Nothing* is as important to your faith as your understanding until you have been shown that your understanding is wrong. Don't just give up on what you believe because somebody says something different than what you believe. Question it. Search it out. And if it's solid…like the Bereans. It's like:

> *"I know Paul, that you've been all over Asia Minor teaching and I've heard about you. Your reputation has preceded you, but I just need to search the Scriptures to make sure that what you're saying is on point."*

The Old Testament contains 39 (Protestant) or 46 (Catholic) or more (Orthodox and other) books, divided very broadly into the Pentateuch (Torah), the historical books, the "wisdom" books and the prophets. Most people in theology say that you have the Old Testament, which is broken down into the Torah, the writings, the Major and Minor Prophets; and of course you have the historical books.

There is no scholarly consensus as to when the Hebrew Bible canon was fixed. I went off to say that this is one of the reasons why I have said that whenever you are reading a letter or a book of the Bible, one of the things that you want to find out is when it was written. That's because if you are fifty years old and you tell me that you knew somebody that died fifty-five years ago, then I can question what you say.

What scholars do and what the canon did was to say:

> *"Okay. Here is a timeline that these books – this is a window in which this book could have been written."*

Depending upon which scholarly group you come under, those numbers may be off a little bit.

When I say that this book was written "between," then there are some timelines, canon or measuring rods that are used to determine what is in the book and what is not in the book. That is also used to determine its historical and spiritual influence. This is why there are books that people want us to read and teach from that have already been denied by most scholars as "not being inspired," but they could be reference materials or historical.

We've got the Apocrypha. Let's just take the Apocrypha. It's in the Catholic Bible, but it's not in the Protestant Bible. These are the books in between the Testaments. Depending upon what denomination you came up in [grew up in], it will determine what Bible you hold as "sacred."

That's because if you're in one of the Protestant churches and they're saying that this is the "infallible word of God" and you have thirty-nine books; over in the Catholic Church they are holding up their Bible. They are saying that this is the "infallible word of God" and it has more books than your thirty-nine.

So whose Bible is "infallible?"

The Catholic Pontifical Biblical Commission says that:

> *"The more restricted Hebrew canon is later than the formation of the New Testament."*

What are they saying? They are saying that there are some folks in the Old Testament that came after the New Testament writings. It is like:

"How is that [possible]?"

That's because just as people determined that the Earth has been around for millions and billions of years, they are using some kind of scientific calculation to determine time. Now, I don't know how all of that stuff works, but I dare say that it boggles my mind to think that men have been roaming the planet for millions of years. It flies in the face of my understanding of creation.

The New Testament is the name given to the second and final portion of the Christian Bible. Jesus is its central figure. The term "New Testament" came into use in the <u>second century</u> during a controversy among Christians over whether or not the Hebrew Bible should be included with the Christian writings as "sacred" Scripture.

Here is where it starts to turn.

The New Testament as we know it today is a collection of twenty-seven books of four different genres of Christian literature (gospels, one account of the *Acts* of the Apostles, Epistles and an Apocalypse, which is *Revelation*).

The first compilation of the New Testament letters or writings only contained a few writings. **Marcion of Sinope was the first to develop what we know of today as a New Testament.** Most of you have never heard of Marcion, unless of course you have gone through my *Discipleship Training* course. (www.Discipleship101.tv)

According to *The New World Encyclopedia,* **Marcion of Sinope** lived from 110-160 C.E. He was a Christian (Catholic) theologian who **was excommunicated** by the early church at Rome **as a heretic.**

Yes, I know I have "Christian" there. You see, I am using *The New World Encyclopedia.* This is the thing about reference

153

materials. There is a way that individuals – we know that they weren't called "Christians" at Antioch, because the word "Christians" didn't exist in the first century. This is a word that came much later. But today's writers, when putting together their reference materials, put words into old literature to make us think that they were always there.

Those of us who know anything about the Catholic Church: it wasn't until the last ten years or fifteen years that the Catholics would even consider themselves to be Christians. They called themselves Catholics. You might say:

> *"Are you a Christian?"*

[They might say:]

> *"No, I'm Catholic! The Christians? They're the Protestants. They're the rebels. They're the ones who jumped out of being Catholic."*

> *"The Catholic is the first church!"*

They're proud about it.

So Marcion was excommunicated. Marcion was deemed a heretic for his rejection of the whole Hebrew Bible and other Christian books that were eventually incorporated into what we know of as the canonical New Testament. He declared that Christianity was distinct from, and in opposition to Judaism.

Notice that he regarded the Elohim of the Hebrew Bible as a lesser *demiurge.* What is he saying? **He's saying that there are two gods in the Old Testament.** This is what – no, no, no, no! [Arthur is responding to the looks on the faces of his audience.]

You see, you don't know! You have all drunk that Kool-Aid. You have bought that. You see, this is where people are when they talk about the God of the New Testament, and some of you all have said it. I hear people praying to Jesus.

[In the past] I started off the day praying differently than I normally pray [now], with what we know of as "the Lord's Prayer." Yeshua said to us that when you pray, what are you to pray?

154

*"Our **Father**."*

Why are Christians praying:

"Lord Jesus..."?

"Lord Jesus?"

You see, praying to him is disrespecting and disobeying HIS command. **That's Marcion-ism!** That's the effect, the impact. You may not know Marcion, but boy have you been influenced by him! He regarded the God of the Hebrew Bible as a lesser *demiurge* and as an angry, wrathful Elohim that was ready to pounce and punish. But the New Testament "God" was a God of love and:

"As long as you 'love,' that's how you know that you're his."

He says that the Elohim that gave the Old Testament was a "source of evil." This is what he said about the Creator! For these reasons his teachings were rejected by the mainstream.

Why? Because he is saying that the Torah, the Law – this is where the folks who reject the Law feel good about rejecting the Law. That's because they're rejecting that God of the Old Testament for the New Testament God who is:

"Jesus Christ Our Lord and Savior, Halleluyah."

Marcion travelled to Rome about 142-143. He arrived in Rome circa 140, soon after Bar Kokhba's revolt. In the next few years he developed his theological system and attracted a large following.

You see, I'm not surprised when I see all of these people running behind "flat Earth" [theory]. I'm not surprised when I see all of these people running behind "round Earth." I'm not surprised when I see all of these people running behind when the day starts. I am not surprised when I see all of these people who are given to conspiracy theories. I'm not surprised when I see all of these people who follow some belief system: a New Moon or a Renewed Moon or a Full Moon.

Why? It's because every theology out there will attract followers. That's every theology. The people who oppose your theology have their own theology. No matter what theology you believe, there will always be people who reject your theology and who have their own. Understand that.

What are they going to do? They are going to spend a lifetime trying to convince you of their theology. Once you get convinced of their theology, *they change theology!* It's like:

> *"You brought me into this and now you've done
> left."*

Yeah. Do you hear what I'm saying? Again, in the next few years, Marcion developed his theological system and attracted a large following. He was a consecrated bishop and was probably an assistant or suffragan of his father at Sinope.

When conflicts with the bishops of Rome arose, Marcion began to organize his followers into a separate community. He was excommunicated by the Church of Rome around 144 and had a large donation of 200,000 sesterces returned.

I just want to take a moment here because the calculation here in that time was calculated as about seven thousand dollars. What Marcion did is what a lot of folks try to do today. They try to buy you. They try to buy churches. They try to buy preachers and pastors.

Politicians are good at it. This is why you will find that practically every politician (especially in this country) – now they have a religious test. Even though a religious test is unconstitutional, that religious test exists.

Of course you can imagine voting for somebody who is not a Christian. There are Messianics voting for people who claim to be Christians, even though they reject their Messianic faith. Are you hearing me, so now today people say:

> *"This is a Christian nation."*

People are wholeheartedly "Christian," even though they are Messianic and don't go to Christian churches. Although they don't go to Christian churches, they still hold onto Christian doctrines and Christian beliefs in their Messianic circles. That makes it easy to buy the line that:

> *"You're Efraim. You're the church. Efraim is the lost sheep of Israel and Judah is your brother."*

So the church is the one house and Jews are the other house. That's where the "two houses" come in. You have all of these teachings and all of these doctrines and a mixture of this and that mixed in with some of that. Pretty soon you have people who are so confused, which is why they can't talk Scripture. They can only talk doctrine. You can listen to some of them and the way they just twist the Scriptures. They just twist them all out of place.

Marcion came in and brought a large donation because he understood "your gift will make room for you." Now the churches take that "your gift will make room for you" as if it's your spiritual gift. Solomon wasn't talking about a spiritual gift! They hadn't been given yet; not like we know them. The Holy Spirit had not been outpoured. Solomon was speaking. He was saying:

> *"Listen. Your gift will bring you before great men. Your gift will make room for you. When you come to meet the king, when you come to meet somebody of authority, you come bearing..."*

What?

> *"gifts."*

Depending on your gift, it will determine your place in line.

Marcion used his personal wealth (particularly a donation returned to him by the Church of Rome after he was excommunicated) to fund an ecclesiastical organization that he founded. Today they're known as "Marcionites."

After his excommunication, he returned to Asia Minor, where he continued to spread his message. He created a strong ecclesiastical organization resembling the Church of Rome and installed himself as bishop.

We don't see that stuff today.

> *"When are you going to make me bishop, bishop?"*

> *"You aren't ready to be bishop yet."*

> *"I am ready to be bishop!"*

> *"I'm not making you bishop yet."*

> *"That's all right. I'll start my own church and I'll be the bishop."*

That stuff doesn't happen today, does it? If you have a disagreement, do you go and start your own congregation and establish your own order? This is what this guy did. This stuff was going on way back then.

According to the development of the canon of the New Testament, Marcion therefore rejected the entire Old Testament. Marcion believed that the twelve apostles misunderstood the teaching of the Messiah. Now, here's somebody who comes years after Messiah and who says:

> *"Those guys didn't understand the Messiah they followed."*

It's amazing to me how somebody can come into the faith, have a few Hebrew lessons, and now they are "experts." They walk around correcting everybody. People you have taught now want to turn around and teach you because you "don't know better." Isn't that amazing? This is what he did.

Marcion believed that the apostles did not understand the Messiah, and holding him to be the Messiah of the Jewish God, falsified his words from that standpoint. In other words, when he read a book of the Bible or a letter and it indicated that the God of the Old Testament was the Father of Yeshua, he rejected that book. That's what he did.

Passages that Marcion could only regard as Judaizing interpolations that had been smuggled into the text by biased editors had to be removed so the "authentic" text of gospel and apostle could once again be available. In other words, he is saying that they were reading into the Bible. Do you know what he did? He did like a lot of preachers do today.

He rewrote the Bible. He rewrote the Bible with his doctrine. Some books that he couldn't rewrite because they were so filled with the Old Testament, he completely denied. After these changes, the Gospel according to *Luke* became the "only" gospel. Luke was a Gentile. Luke was Greek. Luke's gospel was the only gospel that Marcion accepted. That became known as the *Evangelicon*. The ten Pauline letters became known as the *Apostolikon*. He only accepted *Luke* and ten letters of Paul – <u>after he had rewritten them.</u>

Marcion and the Pauline Epistles

Marcion was convinced that among the early apostolic leaders, only Paul understood the significance of Yeshua Messiah or Jesus Christ as the messenger of the Supreme God. *Marcion therefore rejected the entire Old Testament.* He accepted the following writings in this order:

- Gospel according to *Luke*
- *Galatians*
- *1 Corinthians*
- *2 Corinthians*
- *Romans*
- *1 Thessalonians*
- *2 Thessalonians*
- *Ephesians* (which Marion called *Laodiceans*)
- *Colossians*
- *Philemon*
- *Philippians*

These were the only New Testament books that he accepted.

This is a chart that came out of the source *The Development of the Canon of the New Testament.* The symbols here are an indication. You can see these symbols to the left [column].

Symbol	Opinion of Authority
√	accepted; true; scriptural; or quoted from very approvingly
√	possible approving quotation or allusion
√	acceptable, but only with changes
?	dubious; disputed; or useful for inspiration
※	spurious (in the classification of Eusebius)
X	false; heretical; heterodox; quoted from very disapprovingly
·	not mentioned or quoted from; opinion unknown

The chart on the next page shows Marcion here [third entry at the top]. There is Ignatius and Polycarp [column marked "Ig" and "Po"], who were "church fathers." These were disciples of Peter. Then you have Justin Martyr. That's a name you have all probably heard. There are some others, like Irenaeus.

[Please see the chart on the next page.] You'll see that Marcion is this entry in the white [M]. He rejected *Matthew*. He never mentions *Mark*. He changed *Luke*. He rejected *John*. He rejected *Acts*. He changed *Romans*. He changed *1 Corinthians*. He changed *2 Corinthians*. He changed *Galatians*. He changed *Ephesians*. He changed *Philippians*. He changed *Colossians*. He changed *1 Thessalonians*. He changed *2 Thessalonians*. He rejected *1* and *2 Timothy*. He rejected *Titus* and accepted *Philemon,* [but only] *after* he changed it.

	Ig	Po	M	Va	JM	Ir	C	T	MC	O	E	CS	A	D	P	V
Gospel according to Matthew	√	√	X	√	√	√	√	√	√	√	√	√	√	√	√	√
Gospel according to Mark		√		√	√	√	√	√	√	√	√	√	√	√	√	√
Gospel according to Luke	√	√	√	√	√	√	√	√	√	√	√	√	√	√	√	√
Gospel according to John			X	√	√	√	√	√	√	√	√	√	√	√	√	√
Acts	√	√	X			√	√	√	√	√	√	√	√	√	√	√
Romans	√	√	√	√		√	√	√	√	√	√	√	√	√	√	√
I Corinthians	√	√	√	√		√	√	√	√	√	√	√	√	√	√	√
II Corinthians		√	√	√		√	√	√	√	√	√	√	√	√	√	√
Galatians		√	√	√		√	√	√	√	√	√	√	√	√	√	√
Ephesians	√	√	√	√		√	√	√	√	√	√	√	√	√	√	√
Philippians		√	√	√		√	√	√	√	√	√	√	√	√	√	√
Colossians	√		√	√		√	√	√	√	√	√	√	√	√	√	√
I Thessalonians	√	√	√			√	√	√	√	√	√	√	√	√	√	√
II Thessalonians		√	√			√	√	√	√	√	√	√	√	√	√	√
I Timothy		√	X			√	√	√	√	√	√	√	√	√	√	√
II Timothy		√	X			√	√	√	√	√	√	√	√	√	√	√
Titus			X			√	√	√	√	√	√	√	√	√	√	√
Philemon			√					√	√	√	√	√	√	√		√

When you hear people who talk about "Paul, Paul, Paul, Paul, Paul," they're Marcionites. Paul is the only person they refer to. Jesus is "God" and Paul is his apostle, so they pray to Jesus and preach Paul.

Marcion called the writings he approved the *Apostolikon*. For him these became the source, guarantee, and the norm of "true" doctrine. But Marcion removed whatever he judged were interpolations – that is, anything that did not agree with his understanding of what Paul should have written.

[Arthur laughs.] This guy, I'm telling you! Many of you have never heard of him, but you have experienced the impact that he has had on the Christian church.

Although Marcion was excommunicated and his writings rejected, his teachings were influential during the second century and a few centuries after, thus forming a counterpoint to emerging orthodoxy.

The greatest effect that Marcion had on the Catholic Church was this. There are two people who really affected the Catholic Church. Marcion had a major impact, even though they excommunicated him. Another guy that we have come to know was Martin Luther. Martin Luther was actually a Catholic when he died, but he was attributed to the Protestant [Movement] or the "protest-ant" or those who protested the Catholics with his *95 Theses* on the door of the Wittenberg Church in Germany [in 1517].

Martin Luther addressed some issues that were taking place. These were issues that needed to be addressed, but the response was excommunication. Of course this guy Marcion said this. When he began to write these writings – some of us wonder:

> *"Where do Statements of Faith come from? Why do we need to express our Statement of Faith? Why do we need to post 'This is what we believe?'"*

The answer is Marcion. The whole Apostle's Creed, the Nicene Creed, the Athanasian Creed; all of these creeds, the canons adored (the catechisms). Now these guys, because of what Marcion was doing, had to actually begin to establish their doctrine and belief system among their congregants so they would not be pulled or swayed away by this Marcionite-type religion.

Denominations have followed suit. What they have done is create these places called denominations. Now they tag you.

> *"I'm Baptist."*

> *"I'm Methodist."*

> *"I'm Presbyterian."*

> *"Who told you that?"*

> *"Well, I've joined the church."*

How do you join the Baptist Church? Through a *confession of faith*, or through Baptism.

The Marcion effect also did something else. It forced Judaism to no longer orally transmit its teachings. It forced them into writing them out. This is where the Babylonian Talmud and the Mishnah and the Gemara [came along].

Now as Marcion was affecting these Christians (who were also people of Jewish or Hebrew descent), individuals began to look at what was going on and the development of the New Testament. There was pressure now to no longer transmit the oral Torah verbally, but rather to write it down.

Marcion's impact has been great, far and wide. To this day it is still impacting individuals. That is why there are these Statements of Faith.

"This is what I believe..."

It is to the point where when you are sitting down and conversing with somebody from the word and everything they bring up, you can refute with a verse or with a passage or a Scripture; their default response is:

"Well, that's not what I believe."

"Well, what about what the Bible says?"

"That's not what I believe."

That phrase "that's not what I believe" has become the anthem of denominations.

"We don't believe like that."

"We don't believe like that."

"This is what we believe."

There are Statements of Faith. Now you have people who, before they come, want to know:

"Where's your Statement of Faith?"

I can see that in the first century with folks wanting to know.

"Where's your Statement of Faith? What do y'all believe? Why is it not posted? Why is it not written somewhere, where I can see it?"

Marcion played a significant role in the development of textual Christianity by forcing the various churches to

debate the nature of the biblical canon and to delineate its contents.

That, ladies and gentlemen, is the greatest impact that I would say that Marcion had and how that impact is still being felt today.

In the next chapter we're going to go a little bit further. We are going to bring it home, even down to the denominations. We're going to trace the first denomination in America. We're going to see what came over and how it evolved.

Imagine. We read the Bible and there were the Sadducees and the Pharisees. We get the impression that there were some Essenes. Then we understand that there were some individuals who were Zealots. So we've got Pharisees and Sadducees and Essenes and Zealots that we can kind of trace back to the Bible. That's four denominations. Today there are thousands. They are all split, based on disagreements. The split continues.

I thought that when I came into the Hebrew Roots, the Messianic faith, that splits were through. There are just as many splits and denominations amongst the Messianic faith as there are – well, almost. We're not there yet, but it's headed that way.

There are a lot of different doctrines. There are a lot of different teachings. There are a lot of different writings that are now infiltrating the Internet. They are finding their way onto people's computers, laptops and smart devices. They are finding their way into living rooms. I mean, today we stand here in this place at 1334 Hill Road and there are hundreds of people gathered around smart devices, laptops and television screens around the world.

People don't have to come and have fellowship. They can have fellowship from the luxury of their couch or their bed or their bench in the backyard somewhere (unfortunately).

In the next chapter we're going to get into Part 2 of **The Separation of the Testaments and its Impact.** What we saw here was the Old Testament. Then we saw the New Testament and then that separation. We're going to take that a little bit further in the next chapter.

[An audience member asks a question.]

> *"I was wondering whether you were going to address whether the New Covenant and the New Testament were synonymous."*

[Arthur answers.]

Yeah, we will. I wanted to get to it here, because I anticipated that at this point we would do one teaching on this. But the more I went into it, the more I realized that this was not a one teaching deal, so I went to Part 1. But in the next chapter we are going to deal with it. We dealt with this.

There is a teaching that we did on *The Renewed Covenant.* As a matter of fact, we have two teachings [on this], *The Renewed Covenant* and *The New Covenant.* In both of those teachings, we addressed the issue of the New Testament and the New Covenant <u>not being the same.</u>

What we're going to get into is that the New Testament began to be propagated. It began to be taught as if:

> *"This is the New Covenant."*

So by believing the New Testament, people began to believe that they were believing and operating in the New Covenant. We're going to lay that out.

⭑ Part Five ⭑

The Separation of the Testaments and its Impact (continued)

Take what is being said. Analyze what is being said. I believe that if you try and test it in accordance with the Scriptures, that you will find this teaching to be true. If it's true, we have to face it. What happens when we are taught something [new] that goes against what we have been taught [previously]? It becomes somewhat challenging for people to receive because they have to first acknowledge it.

> *"If this is truth, what do I do with it? If this is truth and it is opposed to what I believe, then what I have is not truth, so now I have a decision to make. What do I do with this truth? Do I reject it and continue the way that I have gone? Or do I take it in and acknowledge that what I've held onto for so long is not true?"*

Only the truth makes us free.

We're talking about **The Separation of the Testaments and its Impact**. This is the second half of this portion, which is Part 5 of this book.

In the last chapter I made a statement. I just want to bring some clarification because I misspoke. I said something that was incorrect. I said "AD" was "after death" when "AD" is actually after birth (after the birth of Yeshua). Just to give us some understanding as to letters that are being used:

BCE = Before Common Era

BC = Before Christ

These two are kind of the same, except that one is from a religious perspective and the other is from a secular perspective.

CE = Common Era

AD = Anno Domini (in the Year of our Lord) or after the birth of Yeshua

Of course, they use it as after the birth of "Christ."

The Languages Divided

In this chapter we're going to begin with "The Languages Divided." We're going to look at *John 19*. As I said previously, there's a challenge that I have with this teaching because it's mainly brainy. It's mainly academic, but it's academic that is from Scripture.

Trying to connect academics and Scripture can sometimes be a little boring, but we have to deal with the boring stuff. We have to deal with it because if we don't deal with it, then we may continue on a path that may not necessarily be the right path. Therefore our minds and our understanding need to be renewed.

In *John 19* we see something that can easily be overlooked or ignored. That is, according to *John 19:19-20:*

> *John 19:19-20 – "And Pilate wrote a title, and put it on the cross. And the writing was, JESUS [or Yeshua] OF NAZARETH THE KING OF THE JEWS."*
>
> [20] *"This title then read many of the Jews:"*

In other words, those who passed by saw it.

> *"...for the place where Yeshua was crucified was nigh to the city:"*

People coming in and those coming out saw it. Today it would be like a modern day billboard. You can't miss it.

> *"...and it was written in Hebrew, and Greek, and Latin."*

That's in Hebrew, in Greek and in Latin. If you are looking at another version of the Bible [other than the King James], you may see Aramaic, Greek and Latin. But the languages (Hebrew, Greek and Latin) let us know that these were the languages that were spoken in the day of Yeshua. People spoke Aramaic or Hebrew. People spoke Greek and people spoke Latin.

There were the people who spoke Hebrew and who were of Hebrew origin. Think about this for a moment. There can be a Hebrew who doesn't speak Hebrew. When you're dealing with a Hebrew who doesn't speak Hebrew and you happen to be Hebrew, the question is:

"What's wrong with you?"

Think about this for a moment. If you come from a country where there is a language other than English and you are learned in your mother tongue, you speak to someone who is of your national origin but they don't speak the language. You might think that the person is "lesser than." You may think that they've lost something. Does anybody know what I'm talking about? We have to get this stuff established from day one.

You see, as an "identifiable" African American, the Africans tell me that I shouldn't call myself "African American." They say that I should call myself an American whose descendants are from Africa. Why? That's because I don't speak any African language. The closest I come to any African dialect is *tongues.* [Laughter. Arthur is joking.] That's as close as I come.

So when I'm dealing with people who are a first generation [native speaker] and who have children, I implore to them to:

"Make sure that your children learn your native tongue."

I want you to see this. When the Holy Spirit was given to the children of Israel on the day of Pentecost, the Bible tells us that there were Hebrews from all over the known world. When they came up to Jerusalem, they spoke in their language. They identified themselves and probably gravitated toward the people who spoke their particular language.

But when the brothers and sisters spoke in tongues, the Bible says that they all heard them *in their native language.* It goes on to tell us what their native languages were, based on where they had come from.

This piece here is so important because it sets the foundation of where we are going when it comes down to the separation of the Testaments and its impact. Everything has an origin.

We see here that in the day of Yeshua – who wrote this title? Pilate. Now, Pilate either knew Hebrew, Greek and Latin, or Pilate had some help. Are you hearing me? In the following verse (and we're not going to read that), they came to Pilate and said:

> *"Don't put that like that. He <u>called</u> himself the King of the Jews, but he's <u>not</u> the King of the Jews."*

Pilate said:

> *"Listen. What it is, is what it is."*

We see right here that there are three languages that are being spoken in the day of Yeshua's ministry. **That's very important.** The languages spoken were:

- Hebrew (Aramaic, which is a dialect)
- Greek (Koine)
- Latin

The Israelites who were native to the land spoke <u>Hebrew</u>/Aramaic. The Greeks who were also Israelites spoke Greek (Koine). Then the Romans spoke Latin. The predominant language of the day of Yeshua was Greek. The Romans who were Italians spoke the Latin language.

The word Hebrew there (*"Hebraios"*) is any one of the Jewish or Israelitish nations; in a narrow sense, those who live in Palestine and use the language of the country; all Jewish Christians, whether they spoke Aramaic or Greek. The word is used as "Hebrew" five times.

The word *"Hellenisti"* in Greek is the Greek language. Now, there's *"Hellenisti"* and we're going to see that there's also

"*Hellenistes*" ("hel-lay-nis-tace'") which is a different term, but is in association with the Greeks who spoke the Greek language. Here is what you're going to find about language. Anyone who has literally studied language comes to the conclusion that if you really want to fluently speak the language, you have to immerse yourself in the what? Culture. **Every language has cultural associations.**

Unless you immerse yourself in the culture in which the language is spoken, there are nuances and understandings that are spoken in the language associated with this culture that you won't understand.

Then "Latin" is "*Rhomaisti*" in the Greek. It means: of Rome's strength; the language spoken by the Romans. So the Romans who occupied Palestine (Israel) spoke Latin. The people who lived in the language had been influenced in a huge way by the Greeks, so you had Hebrews who no longer spoke Hebrew. What did they learn? Greek.

Greek in the day of Yeshua would be like English in our day. English is the language of commerce. English is spoken in practically every part of the world. It is the language of commerce [today] whereas Greek was the language of commerce in the day of Yeshua. And Greek was spoken all over the known world. Why? That's because it had been occupied by the Greeks and then by the Romans.

No culture has had a greater influence upon any other culture than the Greek culture.

At the time of Yeshua and the apostles throughout the *Acts of the Apostles*, the New Testament had not been written. And before there was a New Testament, there was the Old Testament, known as the Tanakh. According to the Talmud, much of the Tanakh was compiled by the men of the Great Assembly, a task completed in 450 BCE. It has remained unchanged ever since.

The Tanakh (as we learned recently) consists of twenty-four books. It counts as one book each, *Samuel, Kings, Chronicles* and *Ezra-Nehemiah* and counts the twelve Minor Prophets as a single book. So *1* and *2 Samuel* are not two books. It is one. *1* and *2 Kings* are not two books. It is one. *1* and *2 Chronicles* are not two books. It is one. *Ezra* and *Nehemiah* were one book and all of the Minor Prophets were a single book.

Rabbinic Judaism recognizes the twenty-four books of the Masoretic Text, commonly called the Old Testament, the Tanakh or Hebrew Bible, as authoritative. Modern scholarship suggests that the most recently written are the books of *Jonah, Lamentations* and *Daniel;* all of which may have been composed as late as the second century BCE.

Here we see an evolution.

The Tanakh was translated from what? From Hebrew to Greek. It is what is known today as the **Septuagint** (from the Latin "*septuaginta*" or "seventy"). The Septuagint is Koine Greek. It is a translation of a Hebraic textual tradition that included certain texts which were later included in the canonical Hebrew Bible, and other related texts which were not. As the primary Greek translation of the Old Testament, it is also called the **Greek Old Testament.**

Understand that when the Hebrew text was translated into the Greek, it was not for Gentiles. It was for Hebrews who didn't speak Hebrew. Once Gentiles dominated the Messianic faith, the attempt to separate it from the Old Testament was to separate the Gentiles from the Jews or from Israel.

The New Covenant presented a **huge** problem for those who were powerful men, instrumental in developing the New Testament collection of writings; especially those who were non-Hebrew or not of the House of Israel or the House of Judah.

This is important because we understand that after the Temple of Solomon and the Babylonian captivity, Israel was split into the southern and the northern kingdoms. Now there was the House of Israel and the House of Judah. That was a splitting of the tribes. This carried on for some time. You even had kings of the northern kingdom and kings of the southern kingdom.

During the time of Jeremiah, it was still during the Babylonian captivity. Why were the children of Israel taken into Babylon? It was because they violated the covenant. They broke covenant. One thing you will know about Father is that he is true to his word. He loved Israel, but he spoke to Israel. He said:

> *"As long as you keep these commands, you will remain in the land and you will be fruitful and prosperous. But if you don't diligently hearken to obey these commands that I'm giving you today, then there are some curses that are going to come upon you."*

One of the curses is that they would not be able to remain in the land. They would be taken into captivity. Father didn't deliver the children of Israel from Egypt out of captivity to take them into bondage.

Today some people say that to go under the Law is to go under bondage. But the fact of the matter is that **Israel didn't have the Law when they were delivered.** There was no Moses and Mosaic Law until after they had been brought out of bondage and were given the commandments so they wouldn't have to go back into bondage.

The commands were given to a free people to help them maintain their freedom. But to violate the commands of the free people... *James* says it was the PERFECT Law. It was the Law of Freedom or the Law of Liberty. Israel had a Law that was to keep them from being under bondage to anybody else. The only way they would go under bondage was to violate the commands that had been given. Therefore the Almighty now had to deal with them.

Now you went from the House of Israel to two houses: the House of Israel and the House of Judah, the northern kingdom and the southern kingdom. The southern kingdom was Judah. The northern kingdom was the House of Israel. Here is the problem:

How do you incorporate into this New Covenant that was spoken, those who are of non-Israelite origin?

You see, when people say that the Law was given to the Jews, generally speaking, that is Gentile talk. **The Law wasn't given to the Jews. The Law was given to Israel.** The Law wasn't given to Judah only. The Law wasn't given to the House of Israel only. The House of Israel included all of the tribes when the Law was given. It didn't become split until after they had violated the commands and had gone into bondage.

Now we've got a situation where individuals are trying to determine how non-Hebrew people deal with a covenant that was given to the Hebrew people. That's the big issue right there. The Elohim of Abraham, Isaac and Jacob gave and cut covenant with a people. He gave them the commandments in order for them to keep their part of the covenant.

It was obvious to the scholars engaged in translations of the Hebrew texts into Greek, Latin, and other languages, that the New Covenant was uniquely and specifically Hebrew in origin and needed to be expanded to include all people, especially them.

This task was much easier when the Bible was closely guarded by those who could read the language as the masses of people looked to those who could interpret the languages and teach.

If the Bible is in Hebrew and I'm a Greek speaker (even though I'm Hebrew), I lay claim to something I can't even read. Those Scriptures (as a Hebrew) are for us, but I can't read them. It's another language.

When the children of Israel went into captivity in Babylon, they lost the language. In the translation of *Ezra* and *Nehemiah*, it lets us know that in order for the Hebrew people to understand the Hebrew Scriptures, they now had to be translated from Hebrew into Babylonian. That was because the people had learned the Babylonian language and had forgotten the Hebrew language. Now Ezra has to interpret the Hebrew Scriptures to the Babylonians.

When the Hebrew Scriptures were given, all the people spoke Hebrew. All twelve tribes spoke Hebrew. The thing about captivity is this. Captivity is like prison. Something we kind of do is watch some of these programs about life on the inside to help understand how people think who were once incarcerated.

Someone who has been incarcerated thinks very differently (depending on how long they have been incarcerated) than people who haven't been incarcerated. There is a whole other culture inside the jail. It's a whole other culture inside the prison.

When you are thrust into those environments, you have to learn that culture. The challenge is that being in that culture for so long, you can forget what it was like living outside of the prison. One of the greatest fears of individuals who have been in prison for years and years and years is the fear of not being able to adapt once they are released from prison. This is why the recidivism rates of inmates is high.

The person comes out. Now they have a felony. They can't find a job. They are living with Momma (if they still have a relationship). That's because many of them have cut off and broken off so many relationships and burned so many bridges that people don't want to deal with them anymore. All they have are their skills that they learned in prison, so they know how to live in that environment, but they don't know to live in a free environment.

You see, when Israel was born and brought out of Egypt, they knew how to live as slaves. They didn't know how to live as free people. As soon as situations got difficult, what did they want to do? Go back. It's the same mentality. If you are from a country and its culture is very different than the country that you have come into and things are difficult and you don't speak the language, people are looking at you like you are from Mars.

They don't understand. You don't understand them. They don't understand you. You're eating food they have never seen.

They smell smells they've never smelled before. They're dealing with people they've never had to deal with before.

This is why when people come from one country into America, they gravitate to the section of town where the people from their country live. So now you have "Jewtown" and "Chinatown" and "Little Jamaica." You've got "Russiatown" and "Ukrainiantown." People just gravitate to the culture with which they are most familiar. If they can get into that culture, their survival rate is greater.

When the people were coming into the culture of Scripture, they didn't have access. The [only] access that they had was through people who understood it. They couldn't read it, so they depended upon people to translate and interpret. It was easy as long as people didn't have access. People could control [other] people. People could control folks in religious circles.

Folks [today] don't know their Bible. They come into churches. Because they don't know their Bible, to them, the Bible is a different language (even though it's in English). [Arthur laughs.] When you come in and somebody puts a Bible in your hands and it's a King James Bible and you speak "regular" English, you'll start seeing "Yay" and "thou" and "thither" and "thus." It is like:

> *"What is this, man? Why can't you just write the stuff in plain English?"*

This is what it does. It causes people to now begin to write simpler English translations for simpler English-minded people. I would say that the challenge and the problem is that if you don't have the tools to research the Bible yourself, you're dependent upon the translation. That's no different than if you're dependent upon the person who is preaching and teaching and translating and interpreting what the Bible says.

The Bereans were people who searched the Scriptures. If you don't search the Scriptures, you are easily a target for being misled.

The more the assemblies and later churches took on a more Gentile feel and practice and look, the less Hebrew the Scriptures became until the transformation and evolution was complete.

The congregations which were uniquely Hebrew and Greek-speaking Jews or Hebrews in the first century, have evolved into a predominantly Gentile institution today. The first century congregations were filled with Hebrew people. You can read *Acts* chapters *1, 2, 3, 4, 5, 6, 7, 8, 9* and *10*.

In chapter *10*, the first non-Hebrew person is brought into the mix. The Hebrew people don't know how to deal with this. For the next few years (*Acts 10* through *15*) they said:

> *"Hey. Wait a minute. These Gentiles are coming in by the masses. How do we deal with them? What do we do?"*

That's why we did the teaching on *The First Jerusalem Council: What Do We Do With These Gentiles?* These guys are coming in. They are eating their pork. They're eating their shellfish. They're worshipping a certain way. They're bringing the culture and the customs of their former pagan way of life, right into the assembly. And there they were. They had to deal with them. Imagine. This is what it looks like in our day.

Here you are, a tongue-talking, Holy Ghost, dress-worn-down-to-your-ankles congregation, and somebody comes in who doesn't speak in tongues and who is wearing a dress right above the knee. You've got a problem. Or somebody who is in a Baptist Church is having their Baptist worship and somebody else who comes from a Pentecostal background comes in. During the service while the worship is going on, they start speaking in tongues with the expectation that somebody is going to translate. You've got a problem.

That's because what you have are people who have congregated themselves according to their culture. This is why you have Black Church and White Church and Asian Church and Hispanic Church and African Church. It's because of people.

Our belief systems are incorporated with our culture. The culture of what you believe is displayed. It's on full display in your congregation.

[Arthur uses a stereotype as an illustration.] If you are "hillbillies" and you go to your service, somebody is likely to be playing the banjo and singing with a "twang." Right? To them, that's worship. Now, you're not a banjo-twanging singer, but you come into that "hillbilly" congregation. You look around and it's like:

> *"Man. What in the world are these people doing?"*

In your congregation, you're used to swaying and rocking and singing with "soul." Right? The "hillbilly" comes into your service and says:

> *"What in the world is this mess? That's not worship! There's no twang! Where's the banjo?"*

You would want to show people how to worship, right? Have you ever gone into a congregation where the peoples' music is very different than the music you're accustomed to? It's like:

> *"Maaannnn....*[Arthur checks his watch.] *Whewwww."*

[Laughter] That's because our culture is so much a part of our worship. The thing about it is that our culture is not in the Scriptures, so what do we do? **We make the Scriptures adapt to our culture. Instead of us adapting to Scripture, we force the Scripture to adapt to us!**

This is what has happened! This is why you have all of these [churches]. If you go into some of these churches, they're not even singing in English. You feel out of place. You are out of place among your family members.

New Covenant vs. New Testament

In the first century, the Hebrew Scriptures had to be translated into Greek for the Grecians mentioned in *Acts 6*. It says:

> *Acts 6:1 – "And in those days, when the number of the disciples was multiplied, there arose a murmuring of the* ***Grecians*** *against the* ***Hebrews****, because their widows were neglected in the daily ministration."*

The Grecians are Greek, but the word says more than that they were just Greek. The word says that they are "*Hellenistes,*" one who imitates the manners and customs or the worship of the Greeks and who uses the Greek tongue. So you have a Greek-speaking person who comes into a Hebrew congregation. Now they're speaking Hebrew. They're doing the liturgy in Hebrew.

How many of you have ever gone to a Jewish synagogue and they're speaking in Hebrew while you're there trying to understand and worship? You don't understand, do you? You have no clue. Let me show you something. When people come into the Torah, they are given the idea that they have to now start talking, thinking and acting "Hebraic."

Now they put on kippahs. They are wearing prayer shawls, praying to the east, feeling like they have to learn Hebrew, and that they have to go to Israel. It's like:

> *"Okay. Where did that come from?"*

It's because people believe that:

> *"If we are going to fully evolve into our Hebraic culture and understanding, we have to learn the Hebraic culture."*

Do you know that the Hebraic culture and understanding of Scripture was lost before Babylon? After Babylon, everything became Babylonian. **The greatest impact of the Scriptures and culture has come from the Babylonians.** It came from

179

Babylon. This is why you will find YeHoVaH dealing with Babylon in *Revelation*. It is because:

- The synagogue was established in Babylon.
- The Torah portions were established in Babylon.
- The cycles of reading were established in Babylon...

...Among a people who couldn't even read the Torah.

So when they come from Babylon, it's like:

"Somebody needs to explain this stuff to me because I don't have a clue as to what Ezra and Nehemiah are talking about."

Ezra is looking at this. They've married Babylonian wives. They've learned the culture of the Babylonians. They've learned the language of the Babylonians. They've lost their "Hebraic mindset."

So anything people learned "Hebraically" today has a Babylonian twist. The most popular of the Talmuds is not the Jerusalem Talmud, but the Babylonian Talmud. That's because:

- Babylon has influenced the religion.
- Babylon has influenced the makeup and understanding and culture.
- Babylon has influenced the Scriptures...

...Not so much YeHoVaH's word, but how it has been translated and taught.

Logically, the Greek culture began to be incorporated into the practice of the faith. It eventually won out for the first translations of the Hebrew Scriptures into the Greek language to accommodate the Greek-speaking Hebrews.

Think about this. In Israel, they now have to translate the Hebrew Scriptures into Greek. It wasn't for the Gentiles, folks. It was for the Hebrews who couldn't speak Hebrew.

The more the Greek-speaking Hebrews accepted the good news of the faith, the more the congregations took on a Greek culture. The expansion of the gospel went predominantly into Greek-speaking lands.

The New Testament, by use of the Greek word "*diatheke*" transformed the word "covenant" into "testament."

Here's a change right here. The word "covenant" ("*beriyth*" [covenant]) was translated into the Greek word "*diatheke*" (testament). When the *diatheke* translation was applied [instead of the proper Hebrew word and its definition of covenant), now what was [originally] of Hebrew origin, took on a Greek definition.

The word "*diatheke*" refers to a binding will a person made to ensure proper disposal of goods upon the death of the person making the will. Now get this. Today once you get to a certain age, people ask you if you have done what? Made out your will. The will is called a "last will and testament."

A testament is not a covenant. With whom does your will make a covenant? It says that "this goes to this person," whether that person likes it or not. The person who is on the receiving end hasn't made a covenant with the person who is dying. They have no say. They don't even know that a will exists.

There's no covenant in Scripture where the people who are on the receiving end of the covenant have an understanding of what's in the covenant, because it's an agreement.

> *"The New Testament followed the Septuagint (the earliest Greek translation) in using "diatheke" to translate the Hebrew "beriyth" or covenant. New Testament language is thus Greek with a strong Hebrew flavoring."*
> *– Holman Bible Dictionary.*

The New Testament uses the terms "Testament" and "Covenant" interchangeably; giving both words the same definition. You can look up the word "testament" and find it in the New Testament and you can look up "covenant" and find it in the New Testament. What you won't find in the Old Testament is the word "testament."

So what did the Greek do? The Greek turned the Hebrew into Greek. They turned the Hebrew Scriptures into the Greek Scriptures and gave them [Greek words] Hebrew definitions, separating it from the Hebrew culture. [They gave Greek words Hebrew definitions, thus making the Hebrew "Greek."] Now it's starting to take on a Greek culture.

Again, the New Testament uses the terms "Testament" and "Covenant" interchangeably; giving both words the same definition. Now, please pay close attention to this part. Yeshua makes this declaration.

> *Matthew 26:28 – "For this is my blood of the new **testament**, which is shed for many for the remission of sins."*

Let me ask you a question. What is he talking about?

Is he talking about a covenant, or is he talking about a collection of books that haven't been written?

I'll let you think about that for a moment.

Is he talking about something that had been written that he is now fulfilling?

Or is he talking about something that has yet to be written and which will later be fulfilled?

That's because there was no *Matthew, Mark, Luke* or *John*. There was no *Acts* and *Corinthians* and *Thessalonians*. There was NONE of that! It didn't come for another twenty-five, thirty or forty years!

So was Yeshua speaking about letters? Books? Or was he speaking about a covenant that had already been declared? So when he says:

> *"This is the new testament…"*

Was he holding up a New Testament version of the King James Bible? NO! So how did the New Testament version of the Bible become the "New Covenant?" This is what ignorant and unlearned people do. They swallow stuff hook, line, and sinker because they don't know any better. When people who are teaching us say:

> *"Well, this is the New Covenant..."*

> *"Well, it says 'Testament.'"*

> *"Yeah, Testament and Covenant, that's the same thing."*

Yeah, in the Greek!

Here in *Matthew* it says:

> *Matthew 26:28 – "For this is my blood of the new **testament**, which is shed for many for the remission of sins."*

But in *Hebrews* it says:

> *Hebrews 8:10 – "'For this is the **covenant** that I will make with the house of Israel after those days,' saith the Lord; 'I will put my laws into their mind, and write them in their hearts: and I will be to them a God, and they shall be to me a people:'"*

The words "testament" and "covenant" in the Greek are the same. It is *"diatheke."* Notice what this Greek meaning does. If I'm looking up a word in the New Testament with my Strong's Concordance, I'm forced to conclude that this is a Greek term. Therefore I'm going to apply the Greek definition.

The word(s) Testament/Covenant mean(s): a disposition, arrangement, of any sort, which one wishes to be valid, the last disposition which one makes of his earthly possessions **after his death, a testament or** will; a compact, a covenant, a testament; God's covenant with Noah, etc. It is used twenty times as "covenant" and thirteen times as "testament."

The word "covenant" in the Hebrew (*"beriyth"*) is an alliance or a pledge; between men; treaty, alliance, league (man to man); constitution, ordinance (monarch to subjects); an agreement, pledge (man to man); alliance (of friendship); an alliance (of marriage). It just goes on and on.

You don't make a testament with your wife or your husband. That's because if you made a testament with your wife or your husband, it doesn't take effect until after you're dead! That's the definition, folks. I'm not making this stuff up.

The primary difference between testament and covenant is the definition. The covenant is an alliance, treaty or agreement between two parties. A testament is like a will that a person writes and which becomes valid after their death.

Now we have the Hebrew Bible in the Greek New Testament. You've got the Book of *Hebrews* in the Greek New Testament. So the question is, is the Hebrew Book of *Hebrews* – just think about this from a logical standpoint. Shouldn't it be called the Book of *Greeks*? It's the Book of *Hebrews,* written in Greek.

We have to start thinking about stuff, ladies and gentlemen and put our brains "on" when we're searching the Scriptures. We have to start asking questions. We'll find that a lot of things that we've been given just defy logic. Now, get this.

Yeshua lives. YeHoVaH is eternal. Yeshua was not the New Covenant, but the *mediator.* He was/is the *mediator of the covenant* between YeHoVaH and Israel.

Who was the covenant with? The covenant was between YeHoVaH and Israel. **Yeshua mediated the covenant. He was not the covenant!** The New Testament uses the terms "Testament" and "Covenant" interchangeably; giving both words the same definition. Get this.

A covenant, and more precisely the New Covenant, is that it is made by YeHoVaH with a specific people. Who are those people? Israel.

> *Jeremiah 31:33 – "'But this shall be the covenant **that I will make with**...'"*

Who?

This verse right here is the verse that the Gentile scholars had to figure out how to manipulate. They had to, because if as it is plainly written, that the New Covenant was with the House of Israel, then how is it that people who are not of the House of Israel become part of the New Covenant?

Well, you know, we can pull out a wand and because we're dealing with people who don't know, we can start telling them stuff. And we can begin to replace Israel with the church. We can begin to say:

> *"Well, Jesus is the New Covenant and the New Testament books are the New Covenant. The New Testament books and the New Covenant are for the Gentiles and the Old Testament books are for the Jews."*

Do you get this? **Now you have replacement theology. Now you have Gentiles who believe that they are the "spiritual" Israel.** Therefore YeHoVaH is "no longer" dealing with Israel as a people because now:

> *"We, the followers of Jesus Christ are the 'spiritual' Israel. We are the Israel of God. We are the New Testament believers in Jesus Christ, Praise God!"*

This is the stuff that we were sold. Now, maybe that wasn't in your church, but that's what they sold me and I bought it. I chewed on it and said:

> *"You know, that's got some stink to it."*

I couldn't figure it out. Have you ever eaten something and it just had this tainted taste? That's the way it was, "chewing" in the Christian Church. We'd buy this stuff.

I sometimes go onto *Facebook*. People put stuff on *Facebook*. Everybody and their Momma are preaching now on *Facebook,* so we thought we'd join them. Yeah we did. It's like, why should we let the "heathens" have all the fun with *Facebook*

Live? We can put some <u>real</u> stuff on *Facebook Live* and people can actually learn and grow.

But I'm sitting there and watching and it's like this. I am hearing individuals who today are manipulating Scriptures the way they used to manipulate Scriptures in the days that I was sitting in church but didn't know better. I didn't know that they were manipulating Scriptures then. But now that I know the Scriptures, it's like:

> *"Man! That's a manipulation of Scripture."*

And there are people standing. Nobody has a Bible. There's a guy running [Arthur makes a motion as if he's holding a microphone] and he's talking and he's preaching and he's telling people what to say and everybody is just in on it. It is like:

> *"Do these people know what they are coming into agreement with?"*

They're claiming and pronouncing and declaring things while at the same time they are walking in disobedience to the commandments of YeHoVaH. **They're claiming the promises of Abraham while rejecting Abraham!** They are rejecting the faith.

You see, **Abraham didn't put his faith in Jesus. Abraham put his faith in YeHoVaH.**

Yeshua came to reconnect people to YeHoVaH! This is why he says:

> *"When you pray, don't pray 'Lord Jesus.' Pray 'Our Father...Our Father who are in Heaven.'"*

You see, **we are being reconciled back to the Creator of the universe through Yeshua, our Messiah and brother.** He came and showed us how to walk in the Kingdom of YeHoVaH in the world and he said:

> *"Follow me. Do what I do. Say what I say. Then I'm going to send you out because I'm leaving. Whatever I've told you, whatever I've shown*

186

you, this is what you go and preach. Preach what I've taught you!"

What did he teach from? He taught from the Torah. He taught from the *Psalms.* He taught from the writings and the prophets. What did his apostles teach from? They taught from the Torah. They taught from the *Psalms.* They taught from the writings and the prophets. As a matter of fact, **every disciple of Yeshua was dead before there was a New Testament!**

So they couldn't have taught from the New Testament. And do you know what? People were getting "saved." People were getting healed. People were getting delivered. There was power! That's because **the *true* gospel is a gospel of *power*!** He says:

> *"'...**I will make with the house of Israel**; After those days,' saith YeHoVaH, 'I will put my...*
>
> *"Torah"*

That word "law" in *Jeremiah* is the word **Torah**. My Torah.

> *"'...I will put my Torah in their inward parts, and write it in their hearts; and will be their Elohim, and they shall be my people.'"*

So when Yeshua came and ratified it and said:

> *"This is the blood of the covenant..."*

He was talking about *this* covenant. What does this covenant say? It says that **he's going to put his Torah in your heart!** Oh, don't just take my word for it from *Jeremiah. Jeremiah* says:

> *Jeremiah 31:33-34 – "And they shall teach no more every man his neighbour, and every man his brother, saying, 'Know the LORD:' for they shall all know me, from the least of them unto the greatest of them, saith the LORD: for I will forgive their iniquity, and I will remember their sin no more."*

Hebrews picks it up.

*Hebrews 8:10 – "'For **this is the covenant that I will make with the house of Israel** after those days,' saith the Lord;"*

Isn't that verbatim to what *Jeremiah* says? What is he going to do? In *Hebrews* he says:

"'I will put my Torah into their mind, and write them in their hearts:'"

And who is the covenant made with? The House of Israel. Unless you don't know this, the House of Israel was designed to be a house of prayer for all nations. The intent of YeHoVaH is that all nations will come and worship him. Where? In his house. That's the Gentiles, the Hebrews, all twelve tribes. And guess what? Can I just say something to you?

This is why I say that all Hebrews are not Jews and all Jews are not Hebrews. Abraham was Hebrew, but he was not from any of the twelve tribes. Isaac was Hebrew, but he wasn't from any of the twelve tribes.

Can I take it a step further? Ishmael was Hebrew before the Muslims made him Muslim. He was! Why? He was the son of Abraham. Can I let you in on another secret? All of Keturah's children were Hebrew! None of them were Jewish and none of them were from the twelve tribes. Let your mind sink in on that.

There are Hebrew people that have nothing to do with Israel, but church people will have a problem with that. Why? It's because they don't know their Scripture. When you learn your Scriptures, you're not tossed to and fro by every wind of doctrine or some knucklehead who has learned a few words and read a few books.

*[10] "'For **this is the covenant that I will make with the house of Israel** after those days,' saith the Lord; 'I will put my Torah in their mind, and write them in their hearts: and I will be to them a God, and they shall be to me a people:'"*

So who is the covenant with? Israel. Now, notice something ladies and gentlemen, lest you forget. When YeHoVaH sent Moses into Egypt to deliver the Israelites, was it just Israelites that came out of Egypt? There was a multitude of people that were not Israelites. What did they do? Did they leave and go on in their own direction once they left Egypt? No! They were part of the House of Israel.

This is why YeHoVaH says:

> *"Listen. There's only one Law, not two Laws. There's one Law. Everyone who sojourns among you are to keep the same commands that I'm giving you today and you're not to treat them any differently."*

And do you know what? All the males had to do was to be circumcised. Females weren't required to be circumcised to become part of the Hebrews of the House of Israel. All they did was adhere to the commands of YeHoVaH and the blessings and the benefits of the King of Heaven were for them as well. That was not just for them that came out with them, but whoever joined with them.

You see, the children of Israel knew some stuff. Get this. Remember Isaac's sons when their sister fell in love with this Shechemite? They said:

> *"If you want to become one of us, then all you men need to be circumcised."*

That was fair because that was something that the Almighty endorsed. Even Jacob endorsed it. But when the children used the name of YeHoVaH in vain, they cut covenant and then they broke covenant. That's because the people entered into covenant with them and then they turned on them and killed them.

That was a simple process of becoming part of the House of Israel. It was that simple then and it's even simpler now because Yeshua has given access to Israel, the House of Israel and the Israel of YeHoVaH, the God of Israel and you don't have to become a Jew. You just cross over from death to life and that's faith in Messiah.

Don't think for a moment that because the children of Israel, the Jews of the day had their version of the Torah and their laws and were living their laws and their version of the Torah, that they could see the Kingdom. **They still couldn't see the Kingdom because they were depending upon their belief system, not on the Messiah.**

You can depend on your belief system and not on Messiah.

Some people think:

> *"Well, if I just keep the Sabbath and keep the commands and you know, wear tzitzits and eat cleanly and do all of that stuff, then I'm good to go."*

No! You're not. You might be good to go in Judaism, but faith in Messiah requires first and foremost believing that he is who he says he is and surrendering and living and walking in accordance to how he has demonstrated.

He too had his faith in YeHoVaH! Though he was a Son, yet learned he obedience by the things he suffered.

Who did he call on when he prayed? In his darkest hour, who did he call to?

> *Hebrews 8:11-12 – "And they shall not teach every man his neighbour, and every man his brother, saying, 'Know the Lord: for all shall know me, from the least to the greatest.' [12]For I will be merciful to their unrighteousness, and their sins and their iniquities will I remember no more."*

This is *Hebrews* quoting from *Jeremiah*. It's the same covenant. This is the covenant that Yeshua ratified in his blood.

I'm working on a sermon because I've heard people who have implored me to really deal with this issue of the New

Covenant. We've got a couple of teachings called *The New Covenant* and *The Renewed Covenant.* I'm working on a teaching called *The Better Covenant.* It is really going to expound on it and bring all of this together so that people understand what they're entering into when they're talking about a New Covenant.

Make no mistake about it:

- **The New Covenant is not the New Testament!**
- **The New Testament is a collection of writings that embody and expound on the New Covenant.**
- **It is NOT the New Covenant.**
- **The New Testament didn't exist when the New Covenant was spoken and ratified by Messiah.**

The New Testament is a collection of twenty-seven books of four different genres of Christian literature (gospels, one account of the *Acts* of the Apostles, epistles and an apocalypse, which is *Revelation*).

The first compilation of the New Testament letters or writings only contained a few writings. Marcion was the first to develop what we know today as a New Testament around 140-144 AD. We dealt with Marcion in the last chapter (Part 4).

Marcion was Catholic. His father was the Bishop of Sinope in Pontus, which was a Greek province. Marcion most likely spoke Latin and Greek, being that he was born in a Greek province and was part of the Roman Catholic Church.

About 180 AD, early translations of the New Testament (from Greek into Latin, Syriac and Coptic versions) began. Now, understand that the Hebrew Torah/Tanakh was translated into Greek (which is called the Septuagint). This was before the Common Era, so we know that the Hebrew Scriptures existed and were translated into Greek long before Yeshua was born. We've got that, right?

The first compilation of Scripture was written by a guy named Marcion, but his [version] was rejected. Again, Marcion was part of a Catholic organization who rejected him. So in 195

AD, the name of the first translation of the Old and New Testaments were combined. Now you have both the Old and New Testaments in one cover and it was called the **Old Latin Bible**.

The Latin term was *"Vetus Latina"* ("Old Latin" in Latin), also known as *"Vetus Itala"* ("Old Italian"). What people have to understand is that the Romans were Italians. They were Italians.

The *"Itala"* ("Italian") and *"Old Italic"* are the collective names given to the Latin translations of biblical texts (both Old Testament and New Testament). **There was no Old and New Testament. It was simply one book called the Old Latin Bible.** This existed before the **Vulgate** (the Latin translation produced by *Jerome* in the late fourth century).

Now what do we have?

- We have the Hebrew Scriptures that have been translated into Greek.
- The Latins translated the Greek portion of the Hebrew Scriptures. They don't translate the Hebrew into Latin. They translate the Greek translation of the Hebrew Scriptures into Latin.

Now the Greek culture that has been incorporated through the translation from the Hebrew Bible is carried over into the Latin. Now the Latin [version] has a Greek flavor. Get this?

There is no single *"Vetus Latina"* Bible. Instead, Vetus Latina is a collection of biblical manuscript texts that are Latin translations of Septuagint passages. The Septuagint is from what? It's the Greek translation of what? The Hebrew Scriptures.

Here is what we have, and we started this teaching on this topic. The Hebrew went from Hebrew to Greek to Latin. Then we're going to find that it shows up in Old English. But there's something else that we need to get.

How many of you have been to Bible College? How many of you have been to churches that taught you Bible College stuff?

So [from their perspective] what is the Old Testament written in? Hebrew! Right? And the New Testament is written in what? Greek. Now, get this. If the Hebrews couldn't speak Hebrew and therefore translated the Hebrew to the Greek, shouldn't the Old Testament also be Greek?

I'm trying to engage your brain now. The people who want to rely upon the Greek portion of the Scriptures want to tell us that the Hebrew (which was translated into the Greek) was written in Hebrew, when in actuality it was written in Greek. That's because it was translated from the Hebrew to the Greek so that the people could understand it.

Now, you heard the name *Jerome* mentioned. Jerome came along. This is what is happening. I just put this note.

> NOTE: Since the Scriptures were translated from the Hebrew Tanakh into the Greek Septuagint and are used to make the Scriptures readable for a Greek audience, shouldn't both the Old and New Testaments be handed down to us in Greek or Latin? Why is a Hebrew Old Testament now being taught instead of a Greek Old Testament?

Once the Hebrew was translated into the Septuagint, the Hebrew Scriptures were no longer used. It was the Greek portion of the Hebrew Scriptures which was the Septuagint. This is what was being read. This is what was being used to separate the Hebrew speakers from the Greek speakers and to formalize the separation from Hebrew to Greek. Thus we now find the blank page between the Testaments.

You see, they (Seminarians, Bible Colleges, theologians and scholars) want us to believe that the Hebrew Scriptures were written into the Greek Septuagint. Therefore the Old Latin, which the Roman Catholic Church still uses today, was a portion that was literally translated from the Hebrew into the Greek. What they actually have is a Greek Old Testament and a Greek New Testament.

The Hebrew flavor is kind of still on the Greek, but it's more Greek than it is Hebrew. This is important because we know that the Greeks – you don't associate Greeks with Hebrews. In your mind when you hear "Greek," you don't think "Hebrew."

Now we have to distance ourselves from the Hebrew, but we have to hold onto the Hebrew so that the people can make the distinction between the Hebrew and the Greek. In actuality, the Hebrew portion of the Scriptures is translated into Greek, so why do they want to tell us that the Old Testament was written in Hebrew? In actuality it was translated from Hebrew into Greek. That's because it would not make sense to you and this page between the Testaments wouldn't make sense. If the Old Testament is Greek and the New Testament is Greek, it's just one continual flow.

This is so far in the past. I mean, this was long before people came to America. You see, some people think that America has always been. There was a time when America wasn't America. The land mass of America was here, but it didn't have the name "America" until somebody gave it the name "America," which changed it from the name it was before it became "America."

It's amazing how the people who discovered America discovered some Americans. There were people already here. [Arthur laughs.]

> *"Well, what we'll do is call them 'native' Americans and separate them from the rest of the Americans. We'll deem them as 'heathens' and 'savages.'"*

These were "savages" who knew how to treat their wives. These were "savages" who knew how to treat their children. These were "savages" who knew how to treat the land. These were "savages" who knew how to worship.

These were "savages" who may not have known who to pray to. They could have, but one thing they did know is that they knew how to connect to this Spirit that was greater than themselves and they believed that *all* things were connected. *These* were "savages."

You see, when you want to demonize a people, just call them a "cult." Call them "savages." Call them "uncivilized." Call them "heathens." Call them "unlearned." Call them anything that makes them look like they are "lesser than." This is what man has been doing and will continue to do.

In 380 AD, the Latin Vulgate was translated by Saint Jerome. Now, Jerome did something that made the Catholics say that he was a heretic. This is what he did.

He translated the Old Testament into Latin from the Hebrew, and the New Testament from the Greek. He didn't translate the Old Testament into Latin from the Greek translation of the Hebrew Scriptures. He actually translated the Latin Vulgate from the Hebrew Scriptures, so they rejected his writings because he didn't use the Greek Septuagint.

Jerome was smart enough to learn and to know and to speak and to write the Hebrew language so that he could get an accurate translation. He compared the Latin translation (the Old Latin) with the Hebrew as he wrote it in the Latin from the Hebrew, not from the Greek. He compared the Latin and the Greek and the Hebrew and created what is known as the Latin Vulgate. *That was rejected.*

The Latin Vulgate became the Bible of the Western Church until the Protestant Reformation in the 1500s. Around the 1500s (and before that) was this fellow named Wycliffe. Then in the 1600s the King James came along. There were Bibles that were written, but it was Jerome who had an impact on what we know of today as the Protestant Bible – especially the King James.

The Latin Vulgate continues to be the authoritative translation of the Roman Catholic Church to this day. The Protestant Reformation saw an increase in translations of the Bible into the common languages of the people. Here's where things go sideways.

Every time a new language was translated, it was translated from. Now, if Jerome would have translated the Latin Vulgate from the Greek Septuagint, then the Greek flavor and culture would have been a part of his Latin Vulgate. But his Latin Vulgate was reconnected to the Hebrew origin of the faith.

This is why today you will find that people don't necessarily go and look up a Strong's Concordance for the Greek Septuagint except for in the New Testament. But when you study the Old Testament, you look for the Hebrew renderings and it's because of Jerome. Up until Jerome, everybody was studying the Greek Scriptures.

It is maintained by recent scholars that the Apostle's Creed was drawn up in the Roman Church in opposition to Marcionism (cf. F. Kattenbusch, "Das Apost. Symbol.," Leipzig 1900; A.C. McGiffert, "The Apostle's Creed," New York, 1902).

How many of you have ever heard of the Apostle's Creed? If you came up in any mainline denomination, whether it was Lutheran, Episcopalian, Greek Orthodox or Roman Catholic, then you were going to learn the Apostle's Creed. The Apostle's Creed, "we believe..." is a Statement of Faith. Marcion really forced that ideology.

Now it has taken on a new flavor because every denomination now has its own Statement of Faith. Then every church within the denominations has a Statement of Faith. And now people are looking for statements of faith to find out what you believe before they will join themselves with you; as if reading the Bible is not enough.

What is a Statement of Faith? A Statement of Faith is how we interpret. It is how we believe. A person now associates themselves to a particular group of people based on their own belief system that they already have. When a person has a belief system and they go into an environment, they bring their belief system with them. Whenever they hear something that is opposed to what they already believe, they have some problems.

It doesn't matter whether it's true or not.

"That's not what I believe. This is what I believe."

"This is what I believe."

"This is what I believe."

Well, how did you get your belief system?

"I discovered it?"

How *did* you get your belief system? I'm going to tell you something. There are people who have belief systems and who have not really read the Bible. People were taught their belief systems growing up in their home. Generally your first exposure to a belief system is most likely where you will spend the rest of your life.

What you were exposed to is going to fortify that belief system by taking the Scriptures to fortify and to build on the belief system of the organization already present. In order for you to believe something other than what you already believe, you've got to be exposed to someone who believes a little differently.

If you are never exposed to someone who believes differently than what you believe, you will believe what you believe the rest of your life until somebody challenges your belief. Now you have to defend what you believe.

Marcion challenged the Catholics. You see, here's what the Catholics did. The Catholics withheld the Bible from the common people. Marcion decided:

> *"Hey. This is a great avenue. If the people are listening to the Catholic Church, they don't have access to the Bible. What we will do is take certain portions of the writings and begin to teach these things. And because people don't know any better..."*

He set up a system that was opposed to the Catholics. It's no different than the Methodists who set up a system that is opposed to the Episcopalians. Everybody has their own system and they are taught to stay within the confines of their system. That's because everybody else outside of that system is "headed in the wrong direction."

People aren't intelligent enough (they say and believe) to search and study the Scriptures and to come away with their own understanding and belief based on their own study. **Most people go to the Bible with an already established (set) belief system and they find Scriptures to reinforce what they already believe.**

When you try to break that Scripture down, or you try to show them that:

> *"Hey, you're reading that in English, but you should be seeing the Greek translation."*

> *"Hey, you're reading that in the English, but you should be seeing the Hebrew translation."*

We've already shown that word that we translate from the book because we read English words. We attribute English definitions to a Greek or a Hebrew Scripture.

I don't know how true this is, but it's been reinforced. I've never done it to a woman of Hispanic origin, but I remember. Do you know how we used to tell someone:

> *"Come here!"*

You know, especially if you're a parent or an adult and you're dealing with a child and you want them?

> *"Come here!"*

Have you ever done that to somebody? [Arthur makes a "come here" motion with his index finger.] It's like, what is this [motion]? But people interpret that, right? As a child, you interpret that [motion]. That's sign language. Then I learned that in some cultures, this [motion] is done to summon a prostitute.

Does anybody confer with that? [Arthur talks to his audience.] You? Is anybody here of Hispanic or "Latino" origin?

This is what I was told, so do you know what I did? I stopped. They say:

"You don't do this…"

[Calling someone by waving their index finger in a beckoning motion toward someone.]

"You do this…"

[Wave with your hand palm side down, motioning with your fingers for someone to come forward.]

Does anybody do this [the latter] in their culture to call somebody? Nobody? You do this?

[Arthur is speaking to an audience member and he waves with his hand, palm side up, beckoning them forward.]

But not this?

[Arthur resumes beckoning someone with just his index finger.]

Why don't you do this?

[Arthur is referring to the index finger calling motion.]

Say what? You were not taught to do this? Why? You don't know. Yeah. In our culture we were taught to do this [beckoning with the index finger]. I've seen people do this [calling someone to them palm side down and waving with their hand as previously described]. And I've seen people do this [calling someone forward palm side up].

But I stopped doing this [calling people with his index finger] when I'm dealing with people from outside of English-speaking, American origins. That's because I don't know. That's what I'm saying. If you don't understand the culture of something, you could be offending people without even knowing that you're offending them. So that old expression…

"When in Rome…"

Do what the Romans do. Just don't eat the shellfish!

At one point in America's history, when a person confessed faith in Yeshua, they were given a New Testament and *Psalms* pocket Bible. Later the pocket Bible was reduced to only the Gospel of *John*.

I remember handing out New Testaments. How many of you have ever handed out a New Testament? It's like:

"A New Testament?"

Now imagine that this is your first introduction to faith and you get a New Testament. Then it got down to where we were handing out the Book of *Psalms* with *John*. It was *John* and *Psalms*, as if there were only two books in the Bible! How many of you have ever handed out *John* and *Psalms*? It is like:

"Where is this madness coming from?"

It is coming from people who are trying to simplify. And get this. The wisdom of the *John-Psalms* Bible is that when people come in, they will be exposed to *Matthew, Mark, Luke* and to *Acts* and the letters. But we're going to start them off with *John* and the *Psalms*.

You see, this is the same thing as in the letter in the Book of *Acts* that was written. It says:

> *"Listen. They have Moses read in the synagogue, but let's just write to them these four things. Don't eat meat sacrificed to idols, abstain from blood, abstain from fornication and idols or things strangled. This is what we're going to put on them. When they come in, they will be exposed to more. But for now, John and the Psalms is enough. For now, the New Testament is enough."*

That's because what is going to happen? If we as a people read the Bible like we read the rest of the books we read; how many of us buy a book and start in the middle? Do you know that the Bible is the only book people read that they don't read from the beginning to the end? It's the only book.

Well, that is unless you like picture books. You don't read. You just look at pictures. But the Bible is practically the only book that people buy where they get a hold of it but they don't begin from the beginning. They'll start at *John* or *Acts* or *Matthew* or *Mark* or whatever the case may be or whatever somebody tells them.

Christians, from the very offset of their introduction to the church, are taught only to focus on the New Testament teachings and that the Old Testament was for the Jews and not for the Gentiles.

In the next chapter, we are going to deal with the evolution that is complete. **We're going to look at how <u>what we have today</u>** (I firmly believe) **<u>was prophesied to be that other gospel.</u>**

It's a gospel that separates the Creator from his creation. It has people focused on something other than. We're going to look at the evolution completed. The subtitle again is *The Evolution Completed: The Other Gospel.*

★ **Part Six** ★

The Evolution Completed: The Other Gospel

We are not where we are ultimately going to be. In order for us to ultimately get where he wants us, he has to give us guidance and lead us by the Spirit. He is going to do that. The Bible says that he will speak to his people and his people know his voice.

We are to know and to be in tune with the voice of the Almighty. What better time to speak than when we gather with the expectation that he's going to speak? When we come before him, we come with the expectation that he is not only going to speak, but he's going to speak to you. Halleluyah.

This is part six, *The Evolution Completed: The Other Gospel.*

The *Acts* of the Apostles opens in chapter 1 with Yeshua and his apostles, and closes in *Acts 28* with the Apostle Paul. In the first nine chapters we will find that the apostles of Yeshua (those who were with him and those he gathered after the resurrection and who he commissioned to take the Gospel of the Kingdom to the nations of the world) continued in ministry.

Around *Acts 9* and *10* where Cornelius comes in, Paul has this conversion. Then from *11* forward, it seems to focus more on the ministry of Paul. It closes in *Acts 28* with Paul's ministry. From there ladies and gentlemen, as much as we know about ministry stops. After *Acts 28,* there is no more biblical history of how the ministry proceeded. From that point on what we have is extra biblical material and historical data that tells us how the saints of old continued to take the gospels.

This is one of the reasons why I encourage people to get *Foxe's Book of Martyrs.* It is because it is a continuation on how the gospel spread. Most people who come up in denominational religion have heard a term called the "church fathers." **The church fathers are not individuals who are mentioned in the**

Bible. These are individuals who came after *Acts* had closed out. These are individuals who seem to have surfaced somewhere in the first and then the second and third centuries. **Those individuals are the ones who literally impacted the gospel as we know it today.**

We started out in this series talking about how the gospel has gone through these changes that I've deemed "evolution." We talked about how it started out in a Hebrew setting. Then it was translated into Greek and the culture of the Grecians. Then with the Romans (the Latins), this is where the Roman Catholic Church came into play. Then from the Roman Catholic Church's Latin, we know that the gospel then became Europeanized.

Then from Europe, the gospel came to America. There it became Americanized. Now the gospel has gone full circle. That's what we're going to close with, in this chapter. We looked at *Acts 1* to see that this is where it all started. Then *Acts 28* is where we see that the biblical history ceases.

Chapter 28 is where Paul's life and ministry began to come to a close before he was sent to Rome to be judged by Caesar. In chapter 24 (which we're going to look at here in a minute), Paul is being accused of teaching against the law. He is identified as a ringleader of the sect of the Nazarene.

This is what it says:

> *Acts 24:1 – "And after five days Ananias the high priest descended with the elders, and with a certain orator named Tertullus,"*

This guy was one of those eloquent speakers.

> *"...who informed the governor against Paul."*

> *Acts 24:2 – "And when he was called forth, Tertullus began to accuse him, saying, 'Seeing that by thee we enjoy great quietness,'"*

First he starts flattering him. Great orators flatter. You know? They make you feel good about yourself. They take all of the good stuff and they get you in. And he says:

> *"'...and that very worthy deeds are done unto this nation by thy providence,'"*

...Governor.

> *Acts 24:3 – "'We accept it always, and in all places, most noble Felix,'"*

Now we identify the Governor as Felix.

> *"'...with all thankfulness.'"*

> *Acts 24:4 – "'Notwithstanding, that I be not further tedious unto thee, I pray thee that thou wouldest hear us of thy clemency a few words.'"*

It's like:

> *"We don't want to waste your time Felix, but it's important that you just give us a little time to share with you, a few words to help you understand why we are gathered here today."*

> *Acts 24:5 – "'For we have found this man a pestilent fellow, and a mover of sedition among all the Jews throughout the world,'"*

Like they know what's going on with all of the Jews throughout the world.

> *"'...and a <u>ringleader</u> of the <u>sect</u> of the <u>Nazarenes</u>:'"*

It's amazing how people try to build their case by involving other people.

> *"Oh, it's not just me! It's not just me who believes that and who feels that way! There are many others."*

> *"Well, who are they?"*

> *"Well, I can't violate their confidence."*

Or:

> *"They want to remain nameless."*

You know, it just bugs me to no end when I read the news and they've got an "anonymous" source who is high up in the administration but who is not "authorized" to speak. And yet you have speaking from them. Yeah.

> *Acts 24:6 – "'Who also hath gone about to profane the temple: whom we took, and would have judged according to our law.'"*

Now, a ringleader "*protostates*" is what we find here. Let me just go back and say that this guy was a ringleader of the sect of the Nazarenes. He wasn't just a ringleader. He was a ringleader of a particular denomination. That is what he is saying here. This denomination is the Nazarenes.

Some folks say:

> *"What do we call ourselves?"*

I don't identify per sea with the Nazarenes because of the denomination, the "Church of the Nazarene." And when it says they were first called "Christians" at Antioch, here we see that it's the Jews who gave the followers of Messiah the name "Nazarenes." It wasn't Yeshua [who did this]. We also see in *Acts* where they were first called Christians at Antioch. By whom? We don't know. They were called this. It is not like they called themselves [this name].

Even the term "Jew" was not a term that Jewish people or Hebrew people called themselves. They were called Jews by the Babylonians. But it is amazing how when you have people who are high up or when you have enough people branding somebody with a particular title, people get tired of defending themselves. They just succumb to the title.

> *"Well, you know. It helps people to know who we are."*

Okay. Back in Grand Rapids, Michigan, there were people who were saying that they were Jewish, but they weren't Jewish.

> *"Well, I say that I'm Jewish because it's easy to explain."*

It's like, really? You're lying! [Laughter] That's a flat-out lie!

> *"Are you Jewish?"*
>
> *"Well no."*
>
> *"Then why are you telling people that you're Jewish?"*

So he's a ringleader of the sect of the Nazarenes.

> *Acts 24:6 – "'Who also hath gone about to profane the temple: whom we took, and would have judged according to our law.'"*

The word here "ringleader" ("*protostates*") is one who stands in the front rank; a leader, chief or champion. It is used one time here as ringleader.

The word "sect" is "*hairesis*." It is from where the word "heresy" comes. Interestingly enough, if you search the word "sect," in the King James Bible and the Strong's Concordance, there was the sect of the Pharisees. There was the sect of the Sadducees. So what were they? **Heresy.**

I am pulling this definition from one of the definitions for this word. It says: **a body of men following their own tenets (sect or party)**; of the Pharisees, of the Sadducees, of the Christians; dissensions arising from diversity of opinions and aims. It also means the act of taking, capture: e.g. storming a city; choosing, choice; that which is chosen.

What we just read is almost the same definition of a cult.

The term "cult" usually refers to a social group defined by its religious, spiritual, or philosophical beliefs, or its common interest in a particular personality, object or goal.

The personality of our "cult" is Yeshua!

I'm an under-cult leader. I'm not the cult leader. Yeshua is the cult leader. I'm just an undershepherd, so when people say:

> *"You know, you guys – y'all are a cult!"*

Yeah, we're a cult. That's supposed to be scary. It's like:

"At least we know we're a 'cult.'"

[Laughter]

"You Baptists and you Pentecostals and all of you all who want to call us a cult, did you know that you are a cult too? That's because all of your denominations have a founder whose personality influenced the denomination and who set the rules, guidelines and boundaries and the doctrines of that denomination that have been passed down from generation to generation to generation to generation."

We're all "cults," <u>except that our "cult" is the true "cult."</u> Halleluyah! I just wanted to get that out of the way!

So they were the sect of the Nazarenes. A Nazarene *"Nazoraios"* is "one separated." It comes from the word "Nazarite." Some people get "Nazarene" and "Nazarite" [mixed up] because of the Nazarite vow. A Nazarite vow is not just made by a Nazarite. The Nazarite vow is a vow. A Nazarene is a Nazarite because they come from Nazareth.

It is just like how a Bethlemite is one who comes from Bethlehem. An Israelite is one who is from Israel, so a Nazarene is the title given to Yeshua in the New Testament. It is a name given to followers of Yeshua by the Jews (*Acts 24:5*). Christians weren't called Nazarenes. The name "Christian" came much, much later.

The Nazarenes in the Christian denomination established the Church of the Nazarene. There is a Church of the Nazarene in practically every city that I have lived in. I can say that.

The faith once delivered to the saints had its origin where? In Israel. The faith was distinctively Hebrew, but as the faith made its way from Israel, it began to become less Hebrew in nature and culture and more Greek; then Latin and then European.

Religion came to America from where? It came from Europe. By the time religion reached the shores of America, it had already been Europeanized. It came by Pilgrims. Pilgrims were Protestants. As said before, Martin Luther started the Protestant Movement. He was Catholic, so the Protestants were actually Catholics. Today's Protestants are simply Catholics who rebelled against the Catholic Church.

But instead of rejecting Catholicism, they just rebranded it as Protestantism. They kept Sunday worship and Easter worship. They also kept Christmas worship. They kept the rejection of the commandments and the Laws; which we see from a European perspective, was really Catholic until King Henry VIII.

A King's Influence

We are going to talk a little bit about King Henry VIII. He rejected the doctrine that (based on the Catholic Church), he could not divorce and remarry. The whole rejection of the Catholic Church and King Henry establishing the Church of England was based on the fact that he wanted to have another wife; [permission for] which the Pope denied.

Not only did he go on to have another wife, he went on to have six more. Now, get this. As a king, one could make the argument based on the Torah, that a king could have more than one wife. He just couldn't have many wives (while rejecting the part of Torah that they don't like). It's amazing how people find aspects of the Torah they like and build their doctrine on it, while rejecting the part that they don't like.

This whole idea of marriage and the separation from the Torah led to what we know of today as Catholicism, Protestantism and Christianity (which rejected the commands). They leave themselves open for interpretation of the commands however they choose. This is what causes denominations to separate, because guess what? When you reject the Ten Commandments; part of the commandments is the Sabbath, honoring your parents, not coveting your neighbor's wife and your neighbor's husband, right?

I was thinking about this on my way to service this morning. You know, Malachi, who was Hebrew, should have informed his niece Esther that as a Torah-observant individual, she shouldn't have been the wife of the king whose wife was still alive. He just put her away.

But how many of you know that they weren't Torah-observant? The king, whom Israel was in captivity to, literally controlled the lives of the people in his reign, so she really didn't have much of a choice to reject being the king's wife. But how many of you also know that the Torah forbids a Hebrew to be married to somebody who is not Hebrew? This is one of the reasons why it took awhile for Esther to become canonized. It was because somebody said:

> *"Hey, you know, there's too much stuff going on in Esther for that to be part of inspiration from the Almighty."*

Again, Pilgrims were Protestants. The United States is the first Western country to be established by Protestants. It's the first. As religion evolved in America, it embodied more of the American culture.

America, ladies and gentlemen, at its roots is defiant of religion. Yet America is very religious. This is confusing to some degree, unless it becomes less confusing. Pilgrims came to America, fleeing religious persecution from King Henry VIII of England, who had already rejected the Pope, his "authority," and the Catholic Church. King Henry declared himself head of the Church of England.

If you think this is gone, it still goes on. In England today, Queen Elizabeth is the head of the Church of England. The people who came to America, came from a kingdom. Now, this is the wrong place to be giving a history lesson, but if you don't understand history, you won't understand how you got here and where you're at. The world around us, the church world around us doesn't have a clue about its own history.

So he broke away. He says:

> *"Pope? We reject your authority and we're going to establish our own authority."*

Now, I need you to hear this. He says:

> *"Pope? We're going to reject your authority, and we're going to establish our own authority."*

He didn't say "we." He said:

> *"Pope? I reject your authority and I'm going to establish my own authority. I reject your church and I'm going to establish my own church. I reject your headship and I'm going to declare myself to be the head of my church."*

What the king did was (get this) bring politics and religion together. That's what he did. That's because up until then, there was a separation of church and state. But the king erased the separation and took authority. So now the kingdom of one who was the ultimate political secular leader, also became the ultimate religious leader.

First of all, Pilgrims came. Close behind them were the Puritans. The difference between the Pilgrims and the Puritans is that the Pilgrims were separatists who believed that they needed to reject the Catholic Church altogether and the religion of the king. But the Puritans were looking for ways in which the people could continue to serve under the king, but still have religion. All it needed to do was "purify" and thus the name "Puritan."

The Pilgrims said:

> *"We don't want anything to do with it."*

The Puritans said:

> *"We can have both."*

Then closely behind the Puritans were the Jews, then the Quakers, then the Lutherans and then the Catholics and then the Deists.

Again, the order of those who came to America:

211

1. Pilgrims

2. Puritans

3. Jews

4. Quakers

5. Lutherans

6. Catholics

7. Deists

The interesting thing about the Deists is this. The ones who had the most impact on the governing document of these United States were these guys. Who were they? Deists believe in the existence of God.

> *"Yep. I believe God exists, but he doesn't govern me. Oh yeah, I believe in God."*

They believed on purely rational grounds, without any reliance on revealed religion, religious authority, or holy text. So their faith was a spiritual faith, but they had no text to define its faith. **They were "believers" who rejected the Bible!**

They believe God was the Creator of the universe, but they don't believe that he gave them any instructions on how they were to conduct themselves, so they made it up.

A quote by Albert Einstein, directed to Rabbi Herbert Goldstein in 1929 describes the essence of Deism:

> *"I believe in Spinoza's God, who reveals himself in the lawful harmony of the world, not in a God who concerns himself with the fate and the doings of mankind."*

In other words, God exists, but he's not involved. He exists, but he's not involved. He doesn't talk to us. He doesn't lead us. He doesn't guide us. He doesn't discipline us. We're not accountable to him, but if we believe in him, we should have some accountability to one another. Thus the evolution of the "herd" mentality.

Spinoza was a Dutch philosopher of Sephardi/<u>Portuguese</u> origin. In other words, he was <u>Jewish</u>, but he was Sephardic. He wasn't Ashkenazi. On July 27, 1656, the Talmud Torah congregation of Amsterdam excommunicated Spinoza from the Jewish community. He was just twenty-three years old.

America the Biblical?

Religion has impacted every aspect of American culture and society because religious freedom is embedded in the US Constitution. And get this. Every politician now has to take an oath of office. They must swear an oath to uphold these religious freedoms before taking office. Now, you may say:

> *"Wait a minute. What do you mean 'religious freedoms?'"*

You see, I brought with me, my copy of the US Constitution. [Arthur holds up a folder.] I've read the Constitution of the United States several times. When it comes down to the Constitution, how many of you know that God is in the Constitution? Right? It literally deals with the fact that we hold these truths to be self-evident, that all men are created [equal] and endowed...created by whom? So, at the beginning of the Constitution, they invoked God into it.

Now, whether it is on the state level, the city level or the federal level, before a politician [takes office], they must all swear an oath. They swear to uphold the Constitution of the United States of America or the Constitution of the state or the laws that govern a community or a county.

This is also true even on a development level where there are homeowner's associations. They don't necessarily swear, but they just have to sign that their purpose is to make sure that the rules and regulations of that association are upheld.

But for any public office, a person has to take the oath of office. What is also interesting is that when a person goes to a court of law, they have to swear an oath to tell the whole truth and nothing but the truth or be found to have perjured themselves (which is a criminal offense).

So we see in every aspect of our lives in society, that the idea of God is there. The inclusion of religious freedoms (at the time, Christianity) in the US Constitution has led many to conclude that America is a Christian nation controlled primarily by Christians or at least by those who believe in Elohim.

Under Article 6 of the Constitution:

> *"The Senators and Representatives before mentioned, and the Members of several State Legislatures, and all executive and judicial Officers, both of the United States and of the several States, shall be bound by Oath or Affirmation, to support this Constitution; but no religious Test shall ever be required as a Qualification to any Office or public Trust under the United States."*

In other words, you don't have to be religious because you will not have to pass a religious test. Now, most people don't know that this is in their Constitution. **You see, the Constitution separated itself from Elohim.** And embedded in the Constitution is the ideology of a separation of state. What King Henry joined together, the Constitution separated.

> *"Brother, we didn't come to church to get a lesson on the Constitution."*

Yes you did, you just didn't know it. Hopefully you are going to conclude that this document, although it may have been inspired by individuals who claim a belief in YeHoVaH, wasn't handed down from Heaven. Some people believe that it was.

I'm going to prove and show this to you. Regardless of faith, someone can become a Senator or a Representative or even the President of the United States of America. Ladies and gentlemen, we may live to see a Muslim President. You might not like hearing that, but this Constitution of the United States guarantees it [that possibility].

214

"We haven't had a Muslim President. Y'all stop that mess up in here. Man, just stop it."

The First Amendment to the US Constitution states:

"Congress shall make no law respecting an establishment of religion, or prohibiting the free exercise thereof; or abridging the freedom of speech, or of the press; or the right of the people peaceably to assemble, and to petition the Government for a redress of grievances."

What is it saying? It is saying that any religion that wants to be, has a right to express its faith in these United States of America. That means any religion. People who want to run Muslims and Sikhs and everybody else out, don't have a leg to stand on according to the Constitution of the United States of America. Now, your faith, whatever it is, may say something different, but the Constitution, the document that governs this country, doesn't support it.

Free elections and voting rights have been referred to as a "sacred process" (by our current President) which every American must participate in. The idea was that somebody would interfere in the "sacred process" of elections, but he is only saying what others believe.

You see, one of the things that I like about our current President is that he says what he feels. Other people beat around the bush. Other people say something. They tell you one thing (and he will too), and do something else. It's just that he is just straight-up out with it. [He just says what he means.] He has exposed a lot of things that have gone on for a long time that other people knew were going on, but they just wouldn't say it.

I'll tell you that no matter what people may say, I love a person who says what they mean and means what they say. Don't say one thing to me and do something else, because you become untrustworthy. I won't believe you. If I find you out, you know how we are. If we find that somebody lied to us:

"Lie to me once, shame on you. [Lie to me twice, shame on me.]"

Once a liar, what happens? Now, unless the Almighty [intervenes], the Almighty can change liars. Liars don't enter into the Kingdom. One thing I know. I might have to deal with liars on this side, but on the other side, I can take people at their word.

Again, free elections and voting rights have been referred to as a "sacred process" which every American must participate in. Why? It's because the Constitution guarantees free elections, open elections. At the time, the only people who couldn't vote were Native Americans, the indigenous people, and slaves. [9] And then of course with the Amendments and the Bill of Rights, that all changed, but it changed hundreds of years later.

American history at its core has paved the way for denominations of choice and religious fanaticism. It guarantees the freedom and protection of religions such as Buddhism, Hinduism, Islam, Sikhism and any other religion one can create or invent. Now, you might not like that, but this document gives them the right and the police have to protect them.

It went even further to now deal with not just the rights of religion, but to pursue life, liberty, and happiness. Now the things that the Scriptures call "abominations" are the "rights" of people that are protected by this "sacred" document [the US Constitution]. Now, I know that I'll probably get a couple of emails that say:

"If you don't like it, then go back to Africa!"

I didn't come from Africa! [Laughter] I came from Cleveland, Mississippi! So if I'm going anywhere "back" to any place, it would be to Mississippi, and it's a nice place to be from. Halleluyah!

---

[9] American women also did not have the right to vote (nationally) until 1920 following the decades-long Suffragette Movement.

"Democracy" is a Greek word meaning: "rule of the people" or "the people rule." The structure of democracy is that the people who rule choose leaders to rule on their behalf as their representatives. According to this document, a representative must be twenty-five years old and a citizen for seven years. Did you know that? Most people don't.

Every US Representative and Senator must swear an oath on the Bible to uphold the Constitution. They do not swear on the Bible to uphold the Laws of YeHoVaH. They swear to uphold the laws of men. When the US Constitution was formed, America was perceived to be primarily a Christian country. That has changed. Today people swear an oath on the religious book of their choice.

There is a Hindu in Congress. Tulsi Gabbard became the first Hindu elected to Congress. She took the oath of office on a *Bhagavad Gita,* a seven-hundred verse Hindu scripture. Guess who gave her the oath? John Boehner. That book is not a Bible; at least it's not a Christian Bible. That's a Hindu scripture.

Muslims in Congress include: Rep. Keith Ellison (R) D-MN and Rep. Andre Carson (D-IN). Congressman Keith Elliot was sworn in on Thomas Jefferson's Koran. He was Republican, but is now a Democrat. So the Republicans are giving the oath of office.

John Boehner was the Speaker of the House for the Republicans and who gave the oath of office to this Congressman who was Hindu and it looked like he had no problem doing it; taking pictures and all. It looks like everybody in this picture is smiling. [Arthur shows a photo of Keith Elliot's swearing-in ceremony.] Why? It's because the Constitution of the United States protects this.

You see, Christians and a lot of Messianics have their head somewhere where it doesn't belong. They ignore all of the stuff that they rail against. The Constitution has divided people even though it is designed to bring and to hold people together. Within it you have individuals who can establish parties. There are just rules. Now the primary parties are what? Republicans and Democrats. Both are bound by the same rule of law.

The religious makeup of the Congress today is as in the chart below. There are 241 members of Congress who are Protestants in the House. There are 144 members who are Catholic, twenty-two who are Jewish, seven who are Mormons. I don't know what that "DK/Reformed" is. I think it stands for "don't know." There are seven. There are two Muslims and two Buddhists. There are three Hindus and there is one each Unitarian and Unaffiliated.

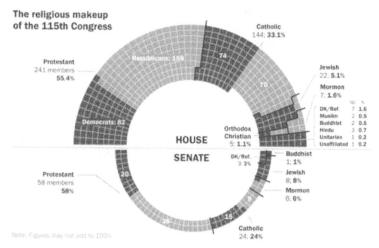

In the Senate are fifty-eight members who are Protestants. There are twenty-four members who are Catholic. There is one Buddhist, eight Jews and six Mormons. These are the people who are writing laws that govern. It is all protected and within the rights of this "sacred" document and they put their hands on whatever religious book they believe to uphold. **Democracy and religion are so intertwined that it is difficult to tell them apart.**

As a democracy and superpower, America is determined to spread democracy around the world. Wherever democracy goes comes the freedom of religion. With the freedom of religion is whatever religion you choose and whatever lifestyle you choose. That's what democracy represents. This is why there is so much opposition against the West.

As some would say, for people who want to destroy America, it is not so much America that they want to destroy as it is the democracy. They want to undermine the democracy. The democracy gives the right, the inalienable right to every individual to live whatever lifestyle they choose. If you discriminate against them, you can be charged. If you commit a crime against them, it is now deemed a "hate" crime.

Today the Bible is being translated into every known language in America and is sent to the nations of the world. Subliminally embedded in the translations are the cultures and traditions of America.

This can explain why wherever the Bible is sent from America, that what comes with it is the freedom to worship and to express one's faith openly. This ultimately leads to the defiance of the government and the attempt to establish democracy where the people desire and want free elections to choose their political leaders.

So when a kingdom rejects Christianity, they're not rejecting faith. Oftentimes they're not rejecting the Christian faith. They're rejecting the democracy that is so embedded within the Christian faith. How many of you know that there are places in Iran where there are Jews and Christians living harmoniously? There are places in Muslim countries where Jews and Christians live.

It's not the faith of the book. It's the culture and the democratic embodiment of the American culture that comes with it. With that embodiment comes a lifestyle of choice. This is why the democracy of the United States of America is concerned about the human rights of other countries; primarily how they treat people of different faiths and persuasions or lifestyle choices. Are you getting this?

The American Gospel has become <u>something other than the Gospel of the Kingdom</u>. The American Gospel is the <u>gospel of denominations.</u>

You may not like it, but it's true. Now there are so many denominations and so many organizations that it is difficult to determine which one is which. Here we come with the Hebrew Roots, which for many really just adds to the number of different belief systems that currently exist in the people who call this Bible "the truth."

This is why I believe so emphatically that Yeshua was saying:

> *"Listen. A new commandment that I give you is that you love one another."*

You see, if I love a person who has faith in Messiah, then it shouldn't matter what denomination they are affiliated with. I am appalled by the fact that there are different denominations who read from the King James Version of the Bible and yet who reject the people of a different denomination who also read from that same King James Version of the Bible. You will have one group who says:

> *"Well, you know, we believe in the whole Bible."*

And there are some groups who say:

> *"No, we only believe in the first part."*

And there are some groups who say:

> *"Well, no, we only believe in the second part."*

And there are some groups who say:

> *"We don't even teach from that."*

There are groups who condemn one type of lifestyle and groups who embrace that same lifestyle that others condemn. So you have all of these denominations with all of these tenets of faith and all of these belief systems. They all come from the same book and supposedly serve the same Elohim!

So, how can you, Mr. Baptist, how can you, Mr. Methodist, how can you, Mr. Pentecostal, hate me and call me names and tell me that I've "fallen from grace," when I read from the same book that you read from?

> *"I ain't hatin' on you! Now, I don't agree with you, but I ain't hatin' on you."*

Many of us have family members. We have family members of various denominations and it's not like we have a real problem with them. They have a real problem with us! We try to hang out with them and they try to slip us up. They try to trip us up every chance they get.

…How to sneak some pork into your food. [Laughter]

> *"Ha ha! You ate some pork! You ate some pork! What does that do now? Should you get stoned?!"*

The fact that you want to establish a standard of morals in an immoral society is something that religious people frown on!

> *"Listen. I don't want to covet your husband. I'm not interested in your wife."*

> *"Well brother, we've got freedom. We're under grace now. We can covet whatever we want."*

Do you hear what I'm saying? I will never forget that a lady wanted me to come into agreement with her and pray. God showed her, her husband. He showed her, her husband, and she wanted me to pray in agreement. As I inquired – some people don't like you asking questions. But you see, I'm not going to come into agreement with something unless I fully understand what I'm coming into agreement with.

> *"Well, you know, I don't want to answer that."*

> *"Well, then I can't help you. Find somebody else to agree with you, because I can't agree with something that I don't know what I'm agreeing with."*

> *"Well, just pray. Just pray with me and I don't want to specify my prayers, but just pray with*

me that the Almighty hears my prayer and answers my prayer."

You want me to pray in agreement that the Almighty hears your prayer and answers your prayer, but you don't want to tell me what your prayer is? How do I know that I'm not praying in agreement with you that God will strike me with lightning? [Laughter] Am I supposed to come into agreement with that?

"Well, if you don't know brother, what's wrong with it?"

What do they call that? An unspoken request.

"I've got an unspoken request pastor. Pray for me!"

I'll pray that YeHoVaH's will be done!

This woman wanted me to come into agreement with her and it's through the inquiry of questions that I came to find out that the husband that God "showed" her was a husband who was married to somebody else! I said:

"Okay. So you want me to pray that God kill that wife so you can marry her husband? Really? What kind of righteous man would I be?!"

Now, if I didn't know the Torah, there would be no problem! I didn't even know the Torah and I knew there was something wrong with that! Halleluyah.

The Cult of Christianity

A Christian denomination is a distinct religious body within Christianity, identified by traits such as a name, an organization, leadership and doctrine. That's a cult. **Christianity is a cult. Islam is a cult. Hinduism is a cult. Buddhism is a cult. They're all cults. Some people just don't like being called a cult.** Why?

"Because it's so "derogatory, brother!"

Well, you know, **the religious leaders in Yeshua's day called him a cult leader.** Why? It was because he was teaching something different than what they were teaching. And get this. *They were cults!* It's like a cult calling a cult a cult!

The gospel which began in Israel has now come full circle and is being sent to Israel from America. Christian Zionism has taken a stand to support Israel and its democracy, which boasts its freedom of democracy and the recognition of its freedom of religion. You may say:

"What's wrong with that?"

I would have to say that according to my understanding of the Bible, YeHoVaH is supposed to be the Elohim of Abraham, Isaac and Israel. He has laid out some specifics as to what is not to be tolerated. I can see why people would want to get rid of the Old Testament, because there are things in the Old Testament that are very difficult to deal with and which hinder one's religious freedom.

You see, if we put our faith in YeHoVaH, who is our Master? I have no more freedom. My freedom is now in Messiah. Messiah becomes my Master. I don't do anything that is opposed to him. I become a slave, a bond servant.

My life is no longer my life. My life belongs to him. I can't say when to go and come. I can't decide what I'm going to do. Now, I do, but I do it with the inquiry of what he wants me to do, to the best of my ability. Whenever I get ahead of him, I've always been able to trust that he is going to correct me. He's going to instruct me. He's going to say something or do something that is going to say to me:

"Arthur? You're going the wrong way."

I remember when we were looking for a facility and I got desperate. I was going to make something happen. He confronted me, saying:

"You know, you're getting ahead of me."

I had to put all of that on hold. I had to kind of let that go. I didn't want to. There are things that he said to me that, you know – my wife and me have gone through some stuff. Before I came to the knowledge of faith, even before I came to the knowledge of faith, I knew that something was wrong with my thinking.

I mean, here I am, a heathen, a straight-up heathen, living a full-blown, heathen life. I was trying to enjoy my heathenism to the fullest, but something in me told me that:

> *"If you divorce your wife, it's going to affect your life and ministry."*

Now, I didn't know where that was coming from. I had no idea. Nobody taught me that stuff. Here I was thinking:

> *"If you divorce, you can't marry again."*

> *"Who is that? Who's talking to me?"*

No pastor told me that. As a matter of fact, the pastors were telling me everything but.

> *"Well, you didn't get married...you weren't a believer."*

That was a good one.

> *"You weren't a believer, so your marriage doesn't count."*

So my children don't count? How do you write off everything that you've done up until that point as not counting? Having the presence of mind – even though we got married in a living room of our apartment, we had a preacher. [Arthur asks his wife a question.]

> *"Wasn't he Muslim?"*

We just knocked on the door across the hall and said:

> *"Hey, we need a witness."*

[Laughter] He says:

> *"Sure brother!"*

Why did we feel that we needed a witness?

"Well, you know. You have to get somebody to sign the certificate."

But why did we feel that we needed a preacher? For me, marriage without a preacher just didn't compute. Why do I need a preacher? It's because I want my marriage to be sanctioned in Heaven. Then preacher, you are going to come around and tell me that my marriage didn't count? Do you know, I was born one day, but it wasn't yesterday!

You see, we have the tendency (whether we know it or not) to discern when we're hearing truth, or not. There are things that we want to hear that we know may not necessarily be from the Almighty, but [people will say]:

"It certainly bears witness with my spirit!"

Some of you all know what I'm talking about.

Your Life Isn't Yours

Several months ago when I did the teaching on *Marriage, Divorce and Remarriage,* I knew that I was going to catch some flack. I knew it. That was one of those teachings that I would much rather have avoided (truthfully), knowing that we have people within our congregation who have been divorced and remarried.

You know? How do you stand up in front of people and teach something that you know that people within the congregation will hear? What are they going to do?

I'm thinking that if I teach this the way he's giving me to teach it, there are some people who will leave. They will walk out! Then they showed up the next week. There are going to be some people who are going to hate this message. They're not going to like it. It's hard for people to separate the message from the messenger, which means that they're not going to like me.

I'm supposed to stand up here and tell people that they have to spend the rest of their lives single or divorced as long as their husband or wife is still alive?

> *"Father, I don't like that position. I don't want to teach that."*

> *"Well, what are you going to teach?"*

Now, get it, believe it or not, there are people who refuse to teach what the Almighty wants them to teach. Instead, they teach what their congregation wants to hear. That's called "itching ears."

> *"How DARE you come up in here! Don't you know that half of your congregation is divorced and remarried? And you are going to come in here and preach THAT message, pastor?"*

You see, **when you are called by the Almighty, your life really isn't your life.** The bottom line is that I know, and you and I are both going to have to stand before the Almighty in judgment. I will have to give an account and I will be judged more harshly. You see, the beauty of being a representative, a teacher of the Almighty is that I'm required to teach what he gives me to teach, but I can't force or make anybody do anything.

My job is to simply give people what he gives me, and that's done. I can love you, even though you've been divorced and remarried. I can love you. It doesn't matter. My job is to love people, not to make decisions based on how they've chosen, knowing that they are going to have to give an account for their decisions.

When their lifestyle is total opposed to the lifestyle that I'm living, then I have to decide whether or not I'm going to be in fellowship with that person.

There is a letter. I'm not going to mention the name, but I feel like I have to read the letter. It reads:

226

"May 25. Approximately three weeks ago, I was listening to a panel of men debate various Hebrew Roots topics, when one of the men referenced a teaching titled 'How to Avoid Messianic Traps' by Arthur Bailey. The quotation was positive, so I decided to locate the YouTube video…"

You see, when you mention things, people go looking for it. That's why I'm careful about what I say and mention and give references to. That's because I know people. The letter continues. Again,

"…The quotation was positive, so I decided to locate the YouTube video and watch it. The teaching was straight-forward, inspirational, informative, palatable and applicable. After the teaching ended, I happened upon another video by Arthur Bailey, titled: 'Marriage, Remarriage and Divorce.' My curiosity was raised for the obvious. I had been married and divorced twice. I was looking forward to the possibility of a third, lasting marriage, so I listened to all six sessions, including the Q & A. I was most interested in the remarriage part…"

"I was horror-struck when the teaching indicated that I could not remarry. Both men are still living. This thrust me into a state of uncertainty and perplexity. I had never heard a teaching like this, ever, and felt some witness was needed, so I introduced the teaching to other Hebrew Roots individuals, of which I am a part. They dismissed the teaching and provided me with Christian websites that countered this teaching…"

"I might have been influenced by the influx of information, except for the fact that several years ago I was standing in the mirror of my

townhouse, checking my attire. An audible voice with precise clarity sounded like it broke through time and space and said to me, 'You will never marry again.' Of course, I rebuked the enemy. I did not want to receive negative faith into my life. For some unknown reason, I cried about what I heard."

"I inquired of others as to whether or not what I had heard was from Elohim or God and there were no real answers. The whole incident was too frustrating for me, so I let it go and went on in my life without an answer. While listening to the YouTube teaching, 'You will never marry again' surfaced for a second time, which made the teaching seem like truth was confronting me."

"I felt relieved because my search for an answer was over. I'm still jolted by the teaching. Although there is no way for me to argue with Scripture, I'm also saddened by this entire teaching. I've stopped praying for a husband and place the dream of remarriage at the Father's feet. This is a real adjustment and all I ask is for the Father to comfort me. And this is my prayer."

When I read this and I was meditating on it, I was thinking about all of the notes that I've taken and words that Father has spoken to me. It was his word to me back in 1981 when I was looking to get rid of my wife that confronted me. Did I want to hear that? No. You see, teachings can be dismissed. We can put teachings out there and people can throw them to the curb.

We can speak truth straight from the mouth of YeHoVaH and people can reject it. You can reject me. You can reject the teachings that I teach. You will never have to stand before me, in judgment. One thing that you may be able to reject in your lifetime but ultimately you are going to have to stand and give an account for is when you stand before the Almighty in judgment.

I said during the teaching, [to remain] in whatever [marital] state you're in. I don't have the authority to tell people what state they're in and blah, blah, blah. But I felt that I could say that, because I'm not in the business of telling people what they can and can't do. That's because I'm not your Master. I'm not your Savior. I didn't shed one ounce of blood for anybody in here. Nobody in here was baptized in the name of Arthur.

It's not my job to follow you around to see if you are living according to the teaching that is presented in this place. I've made it my business to know only what Father wants me to know. Whatever it is that he wants me to know, do you know that he has a way of getting it to me? I don't have to go looking for it. Stuff finds me. I get phone calls. I get emails. No little birdie told me anything.

It was the voice of the Almighty who shares certain things and who uses certain people. That's what he'll do with all of you. Most people make their biggest mistakes by drowning out his voice. Father is telling you that the person that you are hanging out with is not the one.

> *"But I ain't got no other prospects, so I'm going to make it the one."*

> *"Well, maybe I can save them. Maybe I can turn them this way."*

> *"Well, maybe I can convince them. They did say that they'd go to church with me."*

You see, ignoring my voice is probably not going to get you into a lot of trouble, but ignoring his voice can cause some major problems for you. I have yet to counsel people in calamity. I have yet to counsel anybody in calamity that Father didn't warn them before the calamity came. That is not one person! Why?

It's because it's his job to make sure that you know what he has to say to you. It is your job to have ears to hear. It is your job. Even when I wasn't in church, I knew. You all know it. You have been told. You have been influenced. You have been infected and [yet you] knew that what you were about to do wasn't right.

For some reason, you think that didn't apply to you, only to find out that it did. Now you're hurt. Now you're in trouble. Now you're in a mess. The day has come where we need to hear.

I know that when I started pulling out this Constitution of the United States and started talking about what is truth and separating it from all of the falsities that people have been inundated with in religious circles – it is just like the woman who was given the website and religion from the Christian Church to uphold what was being taught. But one thing that she couldn't deny was the voice that she heard.

You can ignore that if you want. This stuff that I'm sharing with you is for your own safety. It's not for me, because I'm not trying to get all involved in your life. I'm really not. Whether we ever have tea together or go out to dinner or go on vacation together is irrelevant. If we do, praise YeHoVaH. I pledge to enjoy your company, as long as you ain't annoying!

The Circle Completed

So the gospel which began in Israel has now come full circle and is being sent to Israel from America. Again, Christian Zionists have taken a stand to support Israel and its democracy, which boasts its freedom of democracy and the recognition of its freedom of religion.

One of the invitations that we received lately was a "Love for Israel" conference that I've been asked to come and speak at. I've accepted. Father is already inspiring me on how to minister to people without offending people. That's because you can minister to people without offending them.

The way that you do that is that you remove your feelings and your emotions and move your personality out of the way. You take on the compassion and the love of Messiah. If you love people, you have no choice but to tell them the truth, but you tell it to them in a manner where they know that it is coming from your heart, by his Spirit.

Today, the land which was established to recognize the Elohim of creation now only has idol temples all over the land, church steeples, high places of worship and Islamic minarets, but NO TEMPLE for YeHoVaH.

They've got a wall – a wall. People go and put notes in it. Then the janitors come along and take the notes. It's like, why do you have to write a note to YeHoVaH and put it in a wall? Some people live for the day that they can get to that wall and put a note in the cracks of the wall – like YeHoVaH reads them!

As a matter of fact, he was standing over your shoulder when you wrote it! All you had to do was stop writing and talk to him, right? They put a note in a wall. And that is so "sacred."

It's like:

"Folks. What are you doing?"

And to deal with that and to touch that [in a teaching]:

"Oh, there you go again! Now you're about to rail on the Jews!"

No! It's not about that. The fact of the matter is that all you have to do is travel around and you will hear calls to worship, but it's not calling or coming from the churches. It's coming from those minarets that are all over the place. Minarets. [Arthur makes the sound of such a call.] You know, it's calling people to pray.

Whole cities of Muslim populations shut down and people pull out their mats and start praying wherever they are. The synagogues are empty. There is no temple. Churches with all of their various denominations are empty.

There are gay pride parades – the largest in the Middle East [in Israel]. Abominations and idol worship have a large temple, a large temple of various denominations. There is Hinduism, Sikhism, Islam(ism), Christian(ism), Judaism and there is no

231

place, no temple for the Almighty to be worshipped. I mean, what does that say about the Holy Land?

The Evolution of the Gospel in America is now being exported to the nations of the world. Now, I wanted to do this teaching, not to bring despair, not to rail or to speak negatively or down, but the people who know their Elohim are supposed to be strong, not bound up in religion. Religion is not what we practice, unless of course it is the true religion, which James speaks about.

When we practice our faith in the manner in which he has given us to practice our faith, we have to be aware of all of the various trappings that are trying to get us to worship something other than the Almighty. And that is **culture**, identity as a people, a specific ethnic group, and pride because of one's heritage. This is what has happened.

Ladies and gentlemen, we have to snap out of that! If we're going to be the purveyors of truth and to take the *true* Gospel of the Kingdom to the ends of the world, understand that there is going to be some persecution that comes from that.

Finally, I want to leave you with this, a *Psalm* of David.

> *Psalms 24:1-2 – "The earth is YeHoVaH's, and the fulness thereof; the world, and they that dwell therein. [2]For he..."*

Who? YeHoVaH.

> *"...YeHoVaH hath founded it upon the seas, and established it upon the floods."*

> *Psalms 24:3-4 – "Who shall ascend into the hill of YeHoVaH? or who shall stand in his holy place? [4]He that hath clean hands, and a pure heart; who hath not lifted up his soul unto vanity, nor sworn deceitfully."*

Psalms 24:5-6 – "He shall receive the blessing from YeHoVaH, and righteousness from the Elohim of his salvation. ⁶This is the generation of them that seek him, that seek thy face, O Jacob. Selah."

Enjoy These And Other Fine Teachings
From Arthur Bailey Ministries

Check out our wide selection of important teachings that are also downloadable for FREE from our ministry website at www.ArthurBaileyMinistries.com. We have books, DVDs, videos, Discipleship and Leadership Training classes and more! Here is a sampling of our most popular teachings:

 28 Blessings of Deuteronomy 28 — This teaching summarizes the 28 blessings of *Deuteronomy 28* and what the blessings look like today. Learn how the blessings manifest and the importance of living a Torah-observant, Spirit-filled life. 4-DVDs. Approximately 5 hours.

 Feast of Firstfruits — In this exciting teaching you will learn what are considered to be the Firstfruits offerings, when they are to be presented and why Firstfruits offerings are so important! You will also learn the prayer that is recited during this vital offering which assures the blessing of prosperity upon those who present their gifts unto YeHoVaH. Approximately 1.5 hours.

 Hear, O Israel — "Hear, O Israel" is a call for ALL of the people of YeHoVaH to hear and to obey his commands. Oftentimes when people hear the word "Israel," they think "Jews." Israel consists of twelve tribes. The Jews are only one of those tribes. In this eye-opening, engaging and life-changing teaching, Arthur Bailey explains in-depth, Yeshua's response and the benefits of what it really means to hear and to obey! Approximately 2.5 hours in a 2-DVD set.

 How To Hear God's Voice — Author and teacher Arthur Bailey shares important biblical truths to help you identify and distinguish the voice of the Almighty from every other voice. Learn why YeHoVaH communicates with his people, why he wants you to hear his voice, how to identify his voice from others, where he most likely speaks to you and so much more! 4-DVDs. Approximately 5.5 hours.

Relationships — Arthur Bailey presents from Scripture how the relationships in our lives must be categorized and prioritized according to their importance. You will learn the kind of relationship the Almighty wants with you, how to categorize and prioritize your relationships according to Scripture, how to identify and rectify wrong relationships and more. 2-DVDs. Approximately 2.5 hours.

 Maximizing Your Talents — Understand the parable taught by Yeshua after sharing with his disciples about the Gospel of the Kingdom being preached to the whole world before the end comes. The parable is about three servants who were given specific talents. What distinguished the wise servant from the wicked servant in this parable was determined by what they did with the talents they had been given. Approximately 1.5 hours.

 Merry Christmas? — Where did Christmas originate? What does the Bible have to say about Christmas and its relationship to the birth of Christ? Is Christmas even in the Bible? Should "Christ" be in Christmas? Is Jesus the reason for the season? How should true believers respond to Christmas? These questions and so many more will be answered in this timeless Christmas message. Approximately 1.5 hours.

 The ReNEWed Covenant — In this teaching Arthur Bailey gives a clear, eye-opening, biblical explanation of what the New Covenant is and with whom it is made. He explains how Jews and Gentiles enter into this covenant and what it means for believers today. You will understand why it is called The ReNEWed Covenant and the significant power that is released within the lives of all who embrace the ReNEWed Covenant. This teaching will change your life forever! Approximately 1.5 hours.

 The Power of the Holy Spirit — Author and teacher Arthur Bailey reveals the prerequisites all believers must meet to be filled with the Holy Spirit and power. What is this power that Yeshua spoke of? Is it still available for disciples of Yeshua today and how can they operate in it? These and many other questions will be answered in this fascinating, informative teaching series. 4-DVDs. Approximately 5.5 hours.

<u>True Biblical Prosperity</u> — What is prosperity? Is prosperity biblical? Is poverty a curse? Can believers be prosperous? What does the Bible teach about prosperity? What is true biblical prosperity? What you believe about prosperity will determine what you can and cannot receive from YeHoVaH. This teaching series will leave you with a wealth of information to help you understand why YeHoVaH wants his people to be *prosperous* and to know what *True Biblical Prosperity* looks like! 4-DVDs. Approximately 5.5 hours.

 <u>You Must Be Born Again</u> — The church world took a conversation Yeshua had with a Pharisee at night, and built powerhouse ministries teaching a gospel message of "salvation" and altar calls. Many sermons have been taught about being "born again" and what it should mean to believers today. But what does *John 3:16* really teach within the context that it is written? Like many other biblical passages, this much-quoted verse is preached in a manner that has become isolated from the context in which it was originally written. Approximately 2.5 hours in a 2-DVD set.

 <u>The New Covenant</u> — When did the New Covenant begin? Arthur Bailey journeys inside the first Jerusalem Council as the Apostles, Elders and Ruach Ha Kodesh (Holy Spirit) "discuss" how to deal with a false teaching circulating among believers. Arthur Bailey is a Spirit-filled, New Covenant minister who boldly teaches the Hebrew Roots of the Christian faith. He removes the confusion from covenants that are as important today as they were long ago. Two episodes.

 <u>The Baptism of the Holy Spirit</u> — Yeshua said in *Acts* 1 verse 5: *"For John truly baptized with water; but ye shall be baptized with the Holy Ghost not many days hence."* In verse 8: *"But ye shall receive power, after that the Holy Ghost is come upon you: and ye shall be witnesses unto me both in Jerusalem, and in all Judea, and in Samaria, and unto the uttermost parts of the earth."* When we are baptized with the Holy Spirit, we receive power and authority to speak for YeHoVaH and to demonstrate his power! In this 4-DVD series learn the true evidence of the baptism of the Holy Spirit and more! A must-have for every true believer who wants to walk in their authority. Over 5 hours of teaching.

The Fall Feasts Of YeHoVaH — A 6-DVD set with over 6.5 hours of teaching. Includes teachings on the Feast of Trumpets/Yom Teruah, Day of Atonement/Yom Kippur, the Feast of Tabernacles/Sukkot and the Last Great Day/Shemini Atzeret. This introduction to the Fall Feasts provides insight and understanding of the prophetic shadow pictures of good things to come and helps us to understand how to celebrate these amazing days in a way that pleases Almighty YeHoVaH.

Now Concerning Spiritual Gifts — A 6-DVD set. Over 6.5 hours. Some suggest that the gifts of the Spirit have ceased operation and that the Law is done away with. Among those who accept and teach that the spiritual gifts of the Bible are still operational today, many have abused and misused these gifts in their assembly; similar to the days of Corinth to whom Paul wrote to correct. This series removes the mystery over manifesting spiritual gifts and empowering believers.

And The Heavens Were Opened — An in-depth, inspiring journey through the feasts of Shavuot, Yom Teruah and Hanukkah. Reveals the importance of these biblical events for today's Spirit-filled believers in Yeshua. Learn about operating in the gifts of the Holy Spirit, the works of Messiah and the rededication of the 2nd temple at Hanukkah. 3-DVDs. About 4.5 hours.

Keeping Torah Living Spirit Filled — Journey inside the first Jerusalem Council. Explore how early leaders through the Ruach Ha Kodesh dealt with false teachings circulating among believers and how they incorporated Gentile converts into the newly formed Messianic community. Deepen your understanding. Strengthen your walk in Yeshua Messiah. 3 episodes in about 1.5 hours.

The Love of God — 4-DVDs. Paul wrote in the Book of Romans, *"But God commendeth his love toward us, in that, while we were yet sinners, Messiah died for us."* God demonstrated his love for us by giving his only begotten son to die for our sins. How can we show our love for God? Journey through the *greatest love story ever written.* Learn what our response to the love of God should be. A true story of love, of overcoming, of victory and of power. Approximately 5.5 hours.

<u>Walking in the Power of the Holy Spirit; My Testimony</u> — Join Arthur Bailey as he shares experiences and unique insights in this perceptive, sometimes hilarious and always instructive journey through his ministry spanning more than three decades. He generously shares his life-changing adventures of discovering and tapping back into the roots of the faith that he has long preached with boldness. As a former pastor and teacher in five different Christian denominations before coming to the true faith of the kingdom of YeHoVaH; his unique story is priceless and required listening for those who desire to enhance their own walk in Torah-obedience and in Yeshua Messiah. About 1.5 hours of teaching.

 <u>And You Shall Love The Lord</u> — The Creator of the universe demonstrated his love for us by sacrificing his only begotten son for the sins of man. The Love of God is a gift! You cannot earn it. You don't deserve it and you can't buy it. How do we demonstrate our love for God? Often when sharing the Gospel of Yeshua (*the gospel Yeshua taught, not the gospel "about Jesus"*), the subject of the "Law" comes up. Yeshua clearly stated that he did not come to do away with or to abolish the Law (*Matthew 5:17*). Yet people still argue that we must only "love" YeHoVaH with all of our heart, mind, soul and strength. Are we doing that? What does this look like? The Bible tells us how YeHoVaH wants us to show our love for him. Find answers to questions that you won't find in religion. About 2.5 hours of teaching on 2-DVDs.

 <u>What Do We Do With Those Gentiles?</u> — Discover how according to *Acts 15*, a major challenge existed which confronted the newly formed Messianic community. Arthur Bailey journeys inside the first Jerusalem Council where the Apostles, Elders and the Ruach Ha Kodesh "discussed" how to deal with false teachings and how to incorporate Gentile converts into the newly formed Messianic community. Jewish believers in Yeshua struggled with transitions from ethnic Jewish religious practices which included non-Hebrew people who were unfamiliar with the rich heritage and traditions formed by the Pharisees and handed down by the Elders. This teaching will deepen and strengthen your spiritual walk in Yeshua Messiah as you learn more about the history of the early called-out ones of faith. 2 episodes.

Messianic 201: "Adding to your Faith" — This is the second in a series of three introductory teachings. Messianic 201 picks up where Messianic 101 "The Essentials" leaves off. In this teaching you will learn the crucial elements that should be added to the believers' faith to keep from falling. This teaching is a must-have for anyone desiring to build their faith in Messiah Yeshua. About 2.5 hours of teaching in a 2-DVD set. Follow up with *Messianic 301 "Perfecting Your Faith."*

Messianic 301: "Perfecting Your Faith – Maturing in Messiah" — Today there is as much confusion about being "Messianic" as there is on certain issues across denominational Christianity . In "Messianic 301: Perfecting Your Faith –Maturing in Messiah ,'" the teaching continues where Messianic 201: "Adding to your Faith" left off. This is the third installment of this phenomenal series which deals with perfecting the faith that we have been given. The series provides essential tools for maturing your faith in Messiah Yeshua. Over 5 hours of teaching on 4-DVDs.

Manifesting the Gift of Healing – A powerful, information and inspiration-packed series to help believers today understand their role as they step out in faith to do the things that Yeshua did...heal the sick and much more! Now you can strengthen your confidence and begin to manifest the gift of healing both for yourself and for those around you. Yes, you *can* do the things that Yeshua said that you can do! In fact, we are to do what he did, and greater things (*John* 14:12). Over 4 hours of clear, concise teachings that will truly bless you, presented in a 7-DVD set.

Let No Man Judge You – Today, whenever the verse from Colossians is quoted:

Colossians 2:16 "Let no man therefore judge you in meat, or in drink, or in respect of an holy day, or of the new moon, or of the sabbath days:"

It is generally coming from a Christian in their defense of not having to keep the Law of YeHoVaH. But what is Paul really saying in *Colossians* 2:16? Find out in this dynamic, eye-opening message by Dr. Arthur Bailey. Approximately 1.5 hours on a single DVD.

Browse our Huge Selection of Teaching Resources

Check out our comprehensive collection of books, book/DVD combos, study tools, gifts and unpackaged teachings. There is something for everyone. Makes terrific gifts as well as study programs and witnessing tools for individuals or church ministries! Here is just a small sampling of our many books and educational materials:

Feast of Firstfruits	How To Hear God's Voice	It's Not Finished	Maximizing Your Talents
Sunday Is Not The Sabbath? (English)	Sunday Is Not The Sabbath? (Russian)	The Feast Of Pentecost	What About Grace?
Leadership Development	To Tithe or NOT To Tithe	The Book of Galatians A 4-Book set!	Discipleship Training

Discipleship Training & Leadership Development Programs

Enroll now in our FREE Discipleship Training and Leadership Development programs! These are the only Messianic Hebrew Roots of the faith programs like them on the planet! Learn more about the true history of the faith once delivered to the saints as you prepare for ministry and leadership services of any kind. The *Discipleship Training program* is our 105-class, 2-year accredited, Seminary-level program. Our 27-class *Leadership Development* course is for ministry and personal enrichment. For all believers regardless of your spiritual walk. All courses and materials are available online. Visit us at:

Discipleship101.tv   **Leadership101.tv**

Shalom!

You have just enjoyed one of the many fine teachings available through Arthur Bailey Ministries. Our full selection of materials are available at:

www.ArthurBaileyMinistries.com

 Are you interested in learning more about the *True Gospel* and how to better communicate the word of YeHoVaH? Arthur Bailey Ministries now offers the world's first Messianic, Hebrew Roots of the Faith **Discipleship Training** and **Kingdom Leadership Development** programs. These exclusive learning opportunities are available in workbook and DVD formats and also online for individual or classroom study. Enroll for FREE today!

Discipleship101.tv   Leadership101.tv

Thank you for your interest in our products and ministry teachings! We invite you to participate in our fellowship services at House Of Israel in Charlotte; through one of our satellite locations, or via the Internet. Please see our web site for our weekly television broadcast schedule and live internet events. We are reaching, preaching, and teaching the *True Gospel of the Kingdom of YeHoVaH to the Whole World.* **We would be honored if you would join us!**

Fellowship Location		**Mailing Address**
House Of Israel		Arthur Bailey Ministries
1334 Hill Road		PO Box 49744
Charlotte, NC 28210	HOUSE OF ISRAEL	Charlotte, NC 28277

Office Phone   **Join us each week for our LIVE broadcasts**
888-899-1479   Thursdays @ 7pm ET • Saturdays @ 11am ET

Please stop in at our ministry website to order any of the DVDs, books and other teaching materials and supplies available at our online store.

www.ArthurBaileyMinistries.com

In addition to placing your order online on our secure website, you may also call in your orders at 1-888-899-1479, or send your check or money order to:

Arthur Bailey Ministries
P.O. Box 49744
Charlotte, NC 28277

Your Support is Highly Appreciated!

Be Blessed in Yeshua Messiah! Shalom!

**Taking the True Gospel
of the Kingdom of YeHoVaH
to the Whole World...**

Made in the USA
Middletown, DE
30 December 2021

57298634R00136